About the Author

Piyush Kumar's passion for storytelling has been a lifelong pursuit, which he now realizes through his debut novel. While completing his MBA, the thought of penning a book never left his mind. After years of ideating and putting his thoughts on paper, he has finally accomplished his dream.

"I Was in Love" is an intriguing contemporary romance novel that explores the complexities of modern-day love through the lens of a dating app. Piyush's writing is emotive and captivating, engrossing readers with every turn of the page. With this book, he hopes to inspire readers worldwide and share his love for the written word.

ACKNOWLEDGMENT

In the intricate weaving of this novel, my heartfelt gratitude extends to those who lent their support, encouragement, and inspiration throughout this journey. To my friends, whose unwavering belief fueled my creativity and kept me going, thank you for being the pillars of strength that every writer needs.

A special note of appreciation goes to Aditi Gupta & Devanshi Panday whose invaluable insights and collaboration played a pivotal role in shaping this narrative. Your contributions have added depth and richness to the story, making it a collaborative masterpiece. Thank you for being a creative companion on this literary adventure. To everyone who shared in the highs and lows of this creative endeavor, your presence has made this novel not just a solitary project but a collective work of art. Here's to the power of storytelling and the magic that unfolds when minds converge to create something truly special.

I WAS in Love

Piyush kumar

PROLOGUE

LOVE IS A COMPLICATED EMOTION, ONE THAT CAN FILL US WITH JOY AND HAPPINESS, BUT ALSO WITH PAIN AND HEARTACHE. IT IS A JOURNEY FULL OF UPS AND DOWNS, TWISTS AND TURNS, AND UNEXPECTED SURPRISES.

This is the story of Paras, a young man who believed he had found his soulmate in Akshi, only to have their relationship come crashing down. He struggled to come to terms with the end of their relationship, and found himself lost and alone.

But through the help of his friends and family, Paras began to find his way back to himself. He explored new interests, met new people, and learned to let go of the past. And just when he had given up on love, fate had a way of bringing him face to face with his past once again

Will Paras be able to find closure with his past and move forward ? Or will he be forever trapped in the memories of a love lost? This is a story about the complexities of love, the power of healing, and the resilience of the human spirit. It is a journey that will take you on a rollercoaster of emotions, leaving you breathless and wanting more. So, buckle up and get ready to experience the twists and turns of Paras' life, as he navigates the ups and downs of love, loss, and redemption.

Table of Contents

"IT IS BOTH A BLESSING AND A CURSE TO FEEL SUCH A DEEP AND PROFOUND LOVE FOR SOMEONE WHO IS NOT MEANT TO BE YOURS. THE HEART YEARNS TO HOLD ON, BUT THE HEAD KNOWS THAT IT IS TIME TO LET GO AND MOVE FORWARD."

A Chance Encounter

"Chance encounters are what keep us going."

- Haruki Murakami (Kafka on the Shore)

Sometimes fate is like a small sandstorm that keeps changing directions. You change direction but the sandstorm chases you. You turn again, but the storm adjusts. Over and over, you play this out, like some ominous dance with death just before dawn. Why? Because this storm isn't something that blew in from far away, something that has nothing to do with you. This storm is you. Something inside of you.

A chance encounter can lead to the meeting of two people who may have never crossed paths otherwise. It can create a sense of serendipity and excitement as two individuals discover their connection and begin to explore their relationship.

Paras woke up early in the morning, the sun barely peeking over the horizon. He could already feel the anticipation building within him for another day of football practice with his friends. Football had always been his passion, and he cherished every opportunity to sharpen his skills on the field. After a refreshing shower, Paras joined his family at the breakfast table. They laughed and shared stories, their lively banter filling the room. Paras loved these moments of connection and felt grateful for the warmth and love that surrounded him. Yet, as he finished his breakfast, an undeniable restlessness crept in. Despite the joy he found in football and the love of his family, he felt an unspoken void. With a thoughtful pause, Paras acknowledged this yearning for something beyond the familiar. Intrigued by the possibility of new horizons, he decided to heed his friend's advice and join Tinder. Though initial hesitation lingered, Paras recognized that venturing beyond his comfort zone held the promise of new experiences and unforeseen opportunities.Paras sat alone in his room, wondering whether or not he really wanted to do this.

Paras sat alone in his room, deep in thought. He decided it was time to have a little chat with himself, a moment of introspection. Recently, a friend had suggested trying out Tinder to meet new people, and it had been an interesting experience so far. Yet, part of him wondered if this was really the right path. Reflecting on his feelings, Paras acknowledged the leap into the unknown. Life was about taking chances and embracing new opportunities, he mused. Maybe this venture could lead to something unexpected and meaningful.

Doubt crept in, though. Paras craved deeper connections, someone to share his passions and dreams with. But what if it didn't work out? What if he was just wasting his time? He knew fear shouldn't hold him back. He'd never know unless he tried. Disappointments were possible, but so was finding something truly amazing. Contemplating his options, Paras realized he shouldn't let fear dictate his actions. It was time to step out of his comfort zone, be open to new experiences, and see where this journey would take him. Success wasn't just about hard work and perseverance. It was about embracing opportunities, taking risks, and being open to the unexpected twists and turns of life. Feeling a surge of gratitude for this moment of clarity, Paras decided it was time to swipe right, put himself out there, and see what unfolded. Who knew? This could be the start of something incredible.

Paras opened the Tinder app and created his profile, carefully selecting his best pictures and crafting a witty bio. He reminded himself that life was what you made it, and that sometimes-taking chances was necessary to find what truly mattered. As he swiped through profiles, he experienced a mix of excitement and uncertainty. Each profile represented a potential connection, a possibility of meeting someone who could fill the void he felt inside. But amidst the sea of faces, one profile caught his attention, Akshi.

There was a sparkle in Akshi's eyes and a warmth in her smile that drew Paras in. Something about her profile made him curious to know more. Paras hesitated for a moment, contemplating whether to swipe right. With a swipe of his finger, he matched with Akshi, much to his amazement. When they started talking, Paras was immediately drawn to her. She was bright, witty, and dedicated to helping others. He was captivated by her and wanted to know more about her. That's when Akshi revealed a shocking fact to him: they had attended the same high school. Paras was taken aback. He'd never met Akshi before, yet they'd grown up in the same town and attended the same high school.

Paras, intrigued, "How come you look so familiar?"

Akshi, playfully, "Hahaha, maybe we went to the same high school," Akshi joked.

Paras: "Wait, did you go to Central High?"

Akshi surprisingly, "Yeah! You too? I was joking about high school"

Paras, genuinely surprised, "No way ! It's quite a surprise to discover that we went to the same high school. How did we never meet before?"

Akshi, sharing the sentiment,"I know, right? It's like we were living parallel lives but never crossed paths."

Paras: "Seriously, it's such a small world. What year did you graduate?"

Akshi: "2018. You?"

Paras: "2016, How did we not meet back then?"

Akshi: "Who knows? Maybe we were just in different circles. But hey, we're here now, right?"

Paras, reflecting, "Yeah, better late than never! It's crazy to think about all the missed opportunities. We probably stood next to each other in the lunch line or sat in the same classroom without even realizing it."

Akshi, reminiscing, "Remember that time in our senior year when our school organized that hilarious talent show? I performed a dance routine, and you were part of the organizing committee."

Paras, realizing, "Wait a minute! You were the one who dazzled the audience with your amazing dance moves? I was backstage running around like a headless chicken, making sure everything went smoothly."

Akshi, reminiscing with a smile, "Oh, I remember that chaos! I thought you were some serious committee guys, always looking so focused. Little did I know you were the mastermind behind the scenes."

Paras, with a hint of playfulness, "Well, I had to keep up appearances, you know? But hey, if only I had known the incredible dancer behind the scenes was you, I would've asked for an autograph."

Akshi, modestly dismissing the idea, "Autograph? Oh please, I'm no superstar. But I must admit, organizing that talent show was one of the craziest and most memorable experiences of high school."

Paras, nodding in agreement, "Absolutely! It was filled with laughter, mishaps, and unforgettable performances. It's funny how we were part of the same event, yet our paths never intertwined."

They realized they had worked in the same department and even attended some of the same parties as they talked more. They had never met before, though. Paras couldn't believe fate had brought them together in such a way. They decided to meet in person

"Let's catch up and grab some coffee, Akshi." "I know a very nice cafe nearby."

"Yeah, let's go tomorrow," she agreed, much to his relief.

They agreed to meet in a nearby café. He entered the coffee shop and noticed Akshi sitting at a tiny table near the window. When Paras first saw Akshi, he was totally taken off. She was even more stunning in person than she appeared in her photographs.

"Wow, she's even more stunning in person than in her

photos," Paras thought, a mix of awe and admiration flooding his senses. The sight of her, right in front of him, stirred a subtle excitement and a touch of nervousness, creating a delightful whirlwind of emotions within him.

As he approached her table, Paras' anxiety kicked in. He felt his uneasiness dissipate as they began to converse. They discovered that they had a lot to talk about because Akshi was so easy to talk to. As they were talking, the waiter approached their table with a warm smile.

"Good evening! I hope you're enjoying your time here," he said politely. "You two make a lovely pair. Are you celebrating a special occasion?"

Akshi and Paras exchanged amused glances, both feeling a little flustered but appreciative of the compliment.

Paras, smiling, responded, "Thank you! We're just friends catching up over dinner."

The waiter nodded understandingly. "That's wonderful. Well, if you need anything, don't hesitate to ask. Enjoy your meal!"

As the waiter walked away, Paras and Akshi looked at each other and chuckled softly, the moment adding a light-hearted touch to their evening.

Paras, amused, "I can't believe the waiter thought we were a couple."

Akshi, still feeling the embarrassment, "I know, right? That was so random for the first time."

Paras, finding humor, "But I have to admit, it was kind of funny too."

Akshi, joining in the laughter, "Yeah, it was. I'm just glad we're comfortable enough with each other to laugh it off."

Paras gazed at Akshi with a warmth in his eyes. "Me too. You're such an amazing person, Akshi. I'm really glad we met."

Akshi's smile widened. "I feel the same way, Paras. You're one of the funniest people I've met, and you know how to make me laugh."

Paras's cheeks flushed with a touch of shyness. "Aww, thanks Akshi. You're pretty hilarious yourself. I think we make a good team."

Akshi chuckled. "Definitely! Who needs a boyfriend or girlfriend when we have each other, right?"

They rapidly became friends and discovered that they had a lot in common. They spent the evening laughing and talking, and before they realized it, the night had passed them by.

Paras, his eyes sparkling with enthusiasm, shared a piece of himself with Akshi. "You know, I love cooking in my free time. Do you like cooking too, Akshi?"

A genuine smile played on Akshi's lips as she responded, "Actually, I do! I enjoy experimenting with different recipes and flavors. What kind of dishes do you like to make?"

Paras, his passion for cooking evident, replied, "I like to make a variety of dishes, but I especially enjoy making Indian food. How about you?"

Akshi's eyes lit up, a shared interest creating a connection. "I like making Italian food, but I'm always open to trying new cuisines. Maybe we could have a cook-off sometime!"

Paras, with a playful glint in his eyes, teased, "That sounds like a great idea. I think I could give you a run for your money in the kitchen."

Akshi laughed, the prospect of friendly competition adding a delightful touch. "Ha! We'll see about that, Paras. But seriously, it's so cool that we have this in common. What else do you like to do in your free time?"

Paras, leaning in as if sharing a secret, confessed, "Well, I also love listening to music. I'm a big fan of classical and old '90s music, but I also enjoy some contemporary artists like Post Malone and Juice Wrld. What about you?"

Akshi's eyes widened with shared excitement. "I'm a big fan of Ed Sheeran, and I also enjoy listening to some Bollywood tracks. Have you been to any concerts lately?"

Paras, his honesty evident, admitted, "To be honest, I'm not much of a concert person, but I would love to attend one someday to experience the vibe."

Understanding his perspective, Akshi nodded in agreement. "I totally get it. I haven't been to a concert in a while, but I would love to see Ed Sheeran perform live one day."

Paras, with a twinkle in his eye, suggested, "Maybe we can go together sometime. It would be a fun outing for us."

Akshi's face lit up with excitement. "I would love that, Paras. You're quickly becoming one of my favorite people to hang out with."

As the night unfolded, Paras and Akshi delved deeper into their shared interests. They discovered a mutual love for books and movies.

Paras, curious about Akshi's reading habits, asked, "What kind of books do you like to read, Akshi?"

Her eyes gleaming with passion, Akshi shared, "I'm a big fan of fiction and non-fiction. And you?"

Paras, revealing a glimpse of his literary preferences, said, "I prefer reading non-fiction books, especially those related to history and science. But I do enjoy reading fiction once in a while, like Harry Potter or Game of Thrones."

Akshi's face lit up with delight. "Oh, I love Harry Potter too! Which house do you belong to?"

Paras, with a playful grin, revealed, "I'm a Gryffindor. What about you?"

Akshi, her eyes dancing with amusement, responded, "I'm a Gryffindor too. It's funny how much we have in common, Paras. I'm really glad we met."

Paras, teasingly, remarked, "Oh, Gryffindor, huh? Looks like we've got some competition here. But don't worry, I'm sure I can out Gryffindor you any day."

Akshi, feigning offense, countered, "Oh, please! I've got the heart of a lion when it comes to bravery and courage. You can't beat that."

Paras, with a mischievous glint in his eye, proposed, "Well, maybe not in Hogwarts, but I'll definitely give you a run for your money in the kitchen. Let's settle this with a cook-off!"

Akshi, accepting the challenge with enthusiasm, declared, "Challenge accepted! Just don't be surprised when my Italian pasta takes you down."

Paras, transitioning to a more serious note, confessed, "But speaking of dissimilarities, I must admit, I'm not much of a Bollywood enthusiast. I prefer the magical melodies of classical music and the timeless beats of the '90s."

Akshi, determined to broaden his musical horizon, playfully responded, "Ah, so you're a music connoisseur, huh? I'll have to introduce you to some Bollywood hits that might change your mind."

Paras, extending his hand for a handshake, declared, "Deal! As long as you promise to give some classic rock a chance. I guarantee it'll rock your world."

Akshi, accepting the challenge with a smile, responded, "Deal! I'm all for expanding our musical horizons. But I'll have you know; I can dance to Bollywood beats like nobody's business."

Paras, intrigued, teased, "Oh, really? Well, I must see this in action. Maybe we should have a dance-off next time."

Akshi, with a playful glint in her eyes, countered, "Ha! We'll see about that. But in all seriousness, it's refreshing to have someone with such different interests. It keeps things interesting."

Paras, nodding in agreement, expressed, "Absolutely! It's the differences that make our friendship so exciting. We learn from each other and discover new things together."

Akshi, raising her coffee cup for a toast, said, "You're right. So, here's to our diverse tastes and shared love for good company. Cheers, Paras!"

Paras, clinking his cup against hers, echoed, "Cheers, Akshi! To friendship and all the delightful adventures ahead!"

Bound to Meet

"Whether it's fate, destiny, or just a series of coincidences, we are bound to meet certain people in our lives. And when we do, they have the potential to change us in ways we never thought possible."

The day began like any other for Paras. He woke up early, energized and ready to take on the day. After his morning run and gym session, he returned home to have breakfast with his family. As he savoured the homemade meal, he felt grateful for the loving and supportive family he had. Once he finished breakfast, Paras retreated to his favourite corner in the house, a cozy nook filled with books. He immersed himself in a captivating novel, losing track of time as he got lost in the world of fiction. But while reading, Paras's phone buzzed, and he noticed a message from Myra. Amid Paras and Akshi's blossoming friendship, there was another significant relationship in Paras's life: his bond with Myra.

Myra, an unexpected muse in Paras's life, stepped into his world through the captivating strokes of an artist's brush. It was a rainy afternoon when Paras found himself wandering through an art gallery, seeking solace in the world of colors and imagination. As he stood mesmerized by a painting that seemed to capture the essence of a storm, Myra, too, was drawn to the same masterpiece. Their eyes met, both captivated by the emotion conveyed on the canvas. Myra, her eyes fixated on the painting, remarked, "The artist truly captured the raw beauty of a storm, don't you think?" Paras, slightly taken aback but intrigued, agreed, and thus began a conversation that transcended the boundaries of the gallery walls.

Paras, genuinely curious, inquired, "So, what drew you to this particular painting?"

Myra, a thoughtful expression on her face, responded, "I suppose it's the way it captures the intensity of emotions, you know? The artist communicates a blend of turmoil and beauty, weaving them seamlessly into a single masterpiece."

Paras, connecting with her perspective, chimed in, "I completely agree. It's like looking into a storm and finding a kind of tranquility within the chaos."

Myra, a spark of enthusiasm in her eyes, exclaimed, "Exactly! It's fascinating how art can evoke such profound feelings. Do you come to galleries often?"

Paras, reflecting on his connection with art, admitted, "Not as often as I'd like, but whenever I need a break from the hustle and bustle of life, I find solace in the world of art and music. How about you?"

Myra, with a genuine smile, shared, "I try to visit whenever I can. There's something magical about immersing yourself in creativity, don't you think?" The conversation unfolded like a gentle dance, each exchange revealing a bit more about the depth of their appreciation for the arts.

Paras, caught in the enchantment of the moment, nodded in agreement. "Absolutely. It's like stepping into another dimension, where everything is open to interpretation."

They explored the gallery together, sharing their interpretations of various artworks, discovering the nuances of each other's perspectives. Myra's insights added layers of meaning to the colors and shapes, transforming the art into a shared experience. Myra "Speaking of interpretation, what's your take on that abstract piece over there?"

Paras, his gaze lingering on the painting, mused, "Hmm, it's open to so many interpretations, isn't it? To me, it seems to represent the complexities of human emotion, each brushstroke telling a different story."

Myra, captivated by his insight, responded, "I love that interpretation! It's amazing how art can speak to us in different ways." There was a shared appreciation in their voices, a recognition of the profound connection they felt with the artwork and, by extension, with each other.

As they delved into discussions about life, love, and the unspoken stories behind the paintings, a unique connection blossomed. Paras "Indeed. And hey, speaking of stories, how about we grab a coffee after this and share a few of our own?"

Myra, her eyes lighting up with genuine enthusiasm, responded, "I'd love that. It's been a while since I've had a good conversation over coffee."

Paras, feeling a sense of connection, declared, "Then it's settled. Let's uncover some more stories together."

The art gallery, initially a backdrop for their encounter, became the canvas upon which their friendship unfolded. As days turned into weeks, their friendship deepened. They exchanged stories of their past, dreams for the future, and everything in between. Myra became Paras's close friend, someone he could share his thoughts and feelings with without any reservations.

One day, as Paras was scrolling through his dating app, he stumbled upon Myra's profile. To his surprise, Myra burst into laughter on the video call. "Caught you, Paras! Didn't expect to see me there, did you?" Paras chuckled, realizing the irony of the situation. What started as a chance meeting at art gallery and endless talks in social media had evolved into a friendship that transcended the artistic & digital realm. Myra and Paras became each other's wingmen, sharing details of their dates, providing advice on relationships, and offering unwavering support during times of heartache. Their friendship was a testament to the belief that some connections are meant to be. Paras and Myra were like two peas in a pod, navigating the complexities of life together. Whether it was celebrating each other's successes or providing a shoulder to lean on during challenging times, they had each other's back. Myra often joked that she was Paras's "relationship consultant," offering insights and perspectives on matters of the heart. Paras, in turn, was Myra's go-to person for anything and everything. Their bond went beyond the superficial; it was a connection of shared laughter, shared tears, and a shared understanding that true friendship knows no bounds.

Intrigued, he set aside his book and opened the message. Myra was always full of mischief and playfulness, and her text was no exception.

Myra, with a playful tone, greeted him, "Hey there, Mr. Bookworm! What's new in your world?"

Paras chuckled at her nickname for him. "Hey, Myra! Just the usual, reading my way through another adventure. What about you? Any exciting plans for the day?"

Myra, with a mischievous glint in her eye, teased, "Oh, you know me. Always up to something exciting! But enough about me. I heard you've been exploring new territories in the dating world. How's that going?"

Paras, feeling a hint of embarrassment, blushed at the mention of his recent Tinder experience. "Well, it's been interesting, to say the least. I did meet someone, and we have a lot in common. We went out for coffee yesterday, and it was nice."

Myra, leaning in with excitement, exclaimed, "Oh, la la! A coffee date, huh? Tell me everything!" The conversation took a turn, becoming a blend of friendly banter and genuine curiosity, as Myra dug for the details of Paras's newfound romantic escapade.

Paras proceeded to share the details of his meet-up with Akshi. He spoke about how they matched on Tinder, discovered they attended the same high school and even worked in the same department without ever crossing paths. He recounted the surprise and delight he felt at this twist of fate that brought them together.

Myra listened intently, eager to hear every detail. "Wow, Paras! That's like something straight out of a movie. I can't believe you two never met before. This could be the beginning of a beautiful friendship!"

Paras nodded, a smile tugging at his lips. "You're right, Myra. For now, I'm enjoying getting to know her. We have plans to meet again today at our favourite café."

Myra, with a teasing glint in her eyes, remarked, "Oh, you sly fox! I see where this is going. Are you interested in her, like, romantically interested?"

Paras hesitated, contemplating Myra's question. "Honestly, Myra, I'm not sure yet. I like her as a person, and we have great chemistry. But I think I want to take things slow and see where it goes. Besides, we have so much to catch up on from high school days; it's like discovering a long-lost friend."

Myra, with a playful tease, "Fair enough, my cautious friend. Just remember, sometimes the best relationships start with strong friendships. But hey, enough serious talk! Go, have fun, and tell Akshi I say hi!"

Paras checked his phone and saw Akshi's text from two hours ago. He quickly replied, agreeing to postpone their hangout to tomorrow. He felt a mix of excitement and nerves as he looked forward to spending more time with her. The next day dawned bright and promising for Paras as he prepared to meet Akshi at their favourite café. He looked forward to continuing their newfound friendship and spending more time getting to know her.

As Paras stepped into the café, the familiar scent of freshly brewed coffee enveloped him, instantly putting a smile on his face. He found a cosy spot near the window and settled in, eagerly waiting for Akshi to arrive. Just as he was about to take a sip of his coffee, a voice called out his name. Paras turned around and was delighted to see Manas, a friend from high school, standing there with a wide grin on his face as he saw Paras and Akshi hanging out with each other.

"Paras, my man! Congratulations on your graduation! You did it!" Manas exclaimed, giving Paras a hearty pat on the back.

Surprised yet pleased to see Manas, Paras returned the grin. "Thanks, buddy! It's good to see you too, long time. What brings you here?" Manas chuckled. "Well, it's a small world, my friend. This café is best known for its coffee so just having it, By the way you remember our high school farewell party?"

Paras furrowed his brows, trying to recall the memories buried deep within his mind. "Yeah, I remember it vaguely. Why do you ask?" Manas's eyes sparkled mischievously. "Well, you see when you left the party early, there was someone, in particular, we were discussing and hoping you'd meet."

Paras's curiosity piqued as he leaned in, eager to hear the rest of the story. "Who was it? Do enlighten me was that, Shakshi."

A sly grin spread across Manas' face looking towards Paras's back window. "No Dude, not Shakshi. It was none other than the girl coming towards the café, Akshi! We were all talking about how you two would hit it off if you had the chance to meet and chat. Wait what is that, Akshi!!!!

Paras, initially surprised, now wore a puzzled expression. "Akshi? Really? This is quite the plot twist, Manas. How on earth did you guys even think of this back then?"

Manas leaned in, lowering his voice as if sharing a classified secret. "Well, my friend, it was a mix of intuition and a little matchmaking mischief. We thought you and Akshi would make a great pair, and she's approaching the café as we speak."

Paras laughs at the unexpected turn of events. "You guys were matchmakers, and I had no clue. And now she's here. (acting that he doesn't know about her arrival) What do I do, Manas? Is this some high school farewell party déjà vu?"

Manas (hesitated) "Chill just act normal, be yourself."

Paras laughing at Manas "Chill dude, she's coming to meet me."

Manas eyes wide open as he was surprised to hear that Paras was here at the café meeting Akshi "Dude, that's surprising you came here to meet Akshi, Now spill the beans. How did you guys end up reconnecting?"

Paras, feeling the weight of Manas's expectant gaze, decided to share the story. "Believe it or not, we met on a dating app. It started as just catching up, but now we're here, meeting in person."

Manas burst into laughter. "A dating app? That's classic! I can already imagine the romantic comedy montage. You guys chatting away on your phones, realizing you know each other, and boom – coffee date!"

Paras joined in the laughter, relieved at Manas's easygoing reaction. "Something like that. But hey, don't go making it more dramatic than it is."

As they bantered about the quirks of modern romance, just then, the café door swung open, and there stood Akshi, her eyes scanning the room until they met Paras' gaze. A smile instantly lit up her face as she made her way toward him.

Akshi approached the table. "Hey, paras! Sorry, I'm a little late," Akshi said, taking a seat across from him. "I got caught up in some unexpected household work."

Paras waved off her apology, his eyes twinkling with excitement. "No worries, Akshi. I'm just glad you're here. I was having a funny conversation with Manas earlier. By the way, Akshi, meet Manas, the high school friend who knew we were meant to meet."

Manas greeted Akshi with a wink. "So, Akshi, how did you manage to charm this guy over here?"

Akshi, always graceful, played along. "Well, Manas, I'm just that charming, I guess. Paras couldn't resist."

Manas chuckled, clearly enjoying the banter. "Alright, you two. I'll leave the love birds catching up with their things. Don't want to interrupt the blossoming romance!"

Paras laughed "It's not that thing Manas. Just make sure that you won't make any rumours in the group."

Manas playfully "Chill buddy, I won't tell anyone about this cute couple reunion story and the couple sitting in front of me."

Paras and Akshi both laughed and said their goodbyes to Manas. As Manas left Akshi started asking Paras what Manas was saying before she was here "Now tell me what Manas was talking about me." Paras leaned in, a mischievous grin tugging at the corners of his lips.

"Well, brace yourself because this might surprise you. Manas revealed that you were at our high school farewell party. "Akshi's eyebrows shot up in surprise, a mixture of confusion and amusement on her face. "Wait, you mean you didn't know?" Paras shook his head, his voice tinged with regret. "No, I had no idea. It turns out that everyone was talking about how we would get along and how great of a pair we would make."

Akshi burst into laughter, covering her mouth with her hand to stifle the giggles. "That's hilarious! We were unknowingly the topic of conversation even before we officially met."

Paras joined in her laughter, feeling a sense of relief and joy wash over him. The revelation lightened the atmosphere and served as an icebreaker between them, erasing any lingering awkwardness. "You know what they say, Akshi, destiny works in mysterious ways," Paras remarked, a playful sparkle in his eyes. Akshi nodded, her laughter subsiding into a warm smile. "Indeed, it does. I'm glad fate brought us together again, this time with the knowledge of our shared past. It feels like the universe is giving us a second chance."

Paras reached across the table, gently placing his hand on top of Akshi's. "I feel the same way, Akshi. It's funny how life works sometimes, but I'm grateful for this opportunity to get to know you better." Akshi laughed and said, "Yeah, I was there, but I didn't get a chance to talk to you either.

It's funny how we ended up meeting each other years later in such a random way. But I'm grateful we've found each other now.

Paras nodded, feeling grateful for the chance encounter that brought them together. "It is. I feel like everything happens for a reason. I'm so glad we're friends now." Akshi smiled warmly at him. "Me too, Paras. You're a great friend to have." Paras nodded in agreement, feeling grateful for their newfound friendship.

They ordered their Coffee and continued chatting about their high school memories and catching up on all that they had missed. They feel like it was destiny that had brought them back into each other's lives. Paras and Akshi talked for hours, reminiscing about their old friends, teachers, and the funny moments they had shared during their high school days. As they sat there, sipping their coffee, they felt like no time had passed since they last saw each other. They felt so comfortable with each other's company that it felt like they had known each other forever.

Akshi suddenly remembered something and said, "Oh, I almost forgot! I have some pictures from our high school farewell party. Let me show them to you."

Paras eagerly leaned in as Akshi scrolled through the pictures on her phone, pointing out all their old classmates and friends. But as she swiped through the images, she paused on one photo and said,

"Hey, this is you, Paras. But I don't remember seeing you at the party that night."

Paras looked at the picture and then back at Akshi with confusion. "What are you talking about? I wasn't at the farewell party. I had to leave early to attend a family function."

Akshi was taken aback. "But Manas said that you were there. He even mentioned you and said that you were looking for me."

Paras, a mix of confusion and curiosity in his expression, asked, "Where am I, show!"

Akshi, pointing towards the corner of the picture, replied, "Look, this one there."

Paras, realization dawning on him, exclaimed, "Oh! Yeah,

that's me, OMG!" His surprise turned into amusement as he saw himself captured in a moment.

Paras was surprised as he saw himself in the photo. He couldn't believe that he had been at the farewell party without even realizing it. He tried to recall that night but couldn't seem to remember anything.

Akshi giggled, "I guess you were having too much fun that night, Paras."

Paras blushed, "I guess so. But strangely, I don't remember anything from that night. Maybe I was too busy saying goodbye to everyone and got distracted."

Akshi smiled at Paras' reaction and said, "It's funny how we were both at the same event and didn't even realize it. I guess fate had other plans for us."

Paras chuckled and replied, "I guess so. But you know what they say, better late than never. "Akshi nodded in agreement, and they both went back to looking at the pictures, pointing out their other classmates and the memories they shared. They talked about how much they missed those carefree days and how much they had grown since then. As they finished looking at the pictures, Paras looked at Akshi and said, "You know, Akshi, I'm really glad that we ran into each other again. It feels like we have so much catching up to do.

Akshi smiled back at him and replied, "Yeah, I feel like we have a lot of adventures ahead of us, and I'm excited to experience them with you."

As soon as they finished their coffee Paras noticed a playful gleam in Akshi's eyes. He knew she was up to something mischievous. Suddenly, she leaned in and whispered,

"Hey, want to play a little game of hide and seek? Let's see if we can hide from that chatty aunty who lives next door to me. She's always catching me at the most unexpected times!"

Paras chuckled at the idea. "Sure, why not? It sounds like fun. But are you sure we won't get into trouble?"

Akshi winked at him. "Don't worry, we'll be like ninjas. She won't even know we're here!" With that, she got up and motioned for Paras to follow her.

They quietly slipped away from their seats and found a perfect hiding spot behind a large potted plant near the entrance. Just as they settled in, they saw the aunty approaching the café. They stifled their laughter, trying not to give away their hiding place. With the chatty aunty temporarily out of the picture, Paras and Akshi seized the opportunity to turn their escapade into a series of mini-adventures. Their strategic hiding spot became their base, and from there, they plotted their next moves.

Akshi whispered to Paras, "I heard she's a regular here, and she's quite the detective. Let's see if we can outsmart her again."

They made a plan to move stealthily through the café, utilizing various hiding spots and blending in with the crowd. Each time the aunty appeared on the scene, they skillfully evaded her, making it a playful game of wits. As they navigated through tables and chairs, Paras was impressed by Akshi's agility and quick thinking. The café transformed into their playground, and the mischievous spark in their eyes reflected the thrill of the moment.

At one point, Akshi suggested, "What if we switch roles? I'll distract her while you sneak around."

Paras nodded, "Sounds like a plan." They executed the switch seamlessly, with Akshi engaging the aunty in a friendly conversation while Paras slipped away to find a new hiding spot.

The chatty aunty, unaware of the duo's game, continued to chat away, sharing stories and laughter with Akshi. Paras, now hidden behind a decorative column, watched the scene unfold with a mixture of amusement and suspense. Their café hide-and-seek adventure continued, turning a casual day out into an unexpected thrill. Each successful evasion brought with it a sense of accomplishment, and the shared laughter between Paras and Akshi. As they sat down, Paras couldn't resist teasing Akshi, "You are a master of hide and seek, Akshi. I almost thought we were invisible back there!"

Akshi laughed, "Well, what can I say? When it comes to evading chatty aunties, I've had plenty of practice!"

Paras raised an eyebrow playfully. "Hmm, I'm starting to think you have a secret life as a spy or something."

Akshi pretended to look serious. "Maybe I do, and maybe I don't. You'll never know!"

They both burst into laughter, feeling a delightful connection and comfort in each other's company. The café atmosphere felt warmer and brighter with their shared laughter. As the day came to an end and they were about to part ways, Paras let his playful side take over once more.

"You know, Akshi, I must say, you're quite the partner in crime. Hiding from aunty detectives and all."

Akshi laughed and replied, "Well, it's all in a day's adventure with you, Paras."

He grinned, "Adventures are always more fun with the right company, and I must say, you're the best company I've had in a long time."

They both successfully evaded the chatty aunty, Paras's phone buzzed with Myra's call, and he hesitated to answer. Akshi, noticing the pause, asked curiously, "Is everything okay?"

Paras, deciding to be transparent, replied, "It's Myra, my best friend. Do you mind if I take this call?"

Akshi, being considerate, said, "Of course not, go ahead."

Paras answered the call, and Myra's cheerful voice echoed through the phone, "Hey, stranger! What's up?"

Paras grinned, "Not much, just out and about. What about you?"

Myra chuckled, "Oh, you know, the usual. Hey, are you with Akshi?"

Surprised, Paras asked, "How did you know? I didn't tell you about the timing when I'll be with her."

Myra laughed, "Your Instagram story, buddy! You seemed to be having a great time. I thought I'd check in and see what mischief you're up to."

Paras glanced at Akshi, who was walking, unaware of the conversation content. "Yeah, we're hanging out. Anything specific you called for?"

Myra, in her playful tone, teased, "Oh, no reason. Just wanted to make sure my best friend isn't ditching me for a new BFF."

Paras laughed, "You're irreplaceable, Myra. Don't worry, I'll always have time for you."

Myra responded, "Good to know. Have fun, you two. But, remember, we have an Art gallery visit planned this weekend, and you better not bail!"

Paras assured her, "Wouldn't miss it for the world. Catch you later, Myra."

As he ended the call, Paras couldn't help but feel fortunate to have such understanding friends. He turned to Akshi, who was looking at him with a smile. "Everything alright?" she asked.

Paras nodded, "Yeah, just Myra making sure I don't forget our art gallery visit this weekend. She's a bit possessive about our gallery visits."

Akshi, attempting to keep her tone nonchalant, "She seemed like more than just a friend from your conversation."

Paras, sensing a hint of suspicion, explained, "Myra is my best friend. We've known each other for a long time. Nothing more than that."

Akshi, trying to mask her unease, nodded, "Ah, I see. Just making sure. It's nice to have good friends."

Deep down, she grappled with a mix of emotions. She found herself unexpectedly bothered by the thought of Paras having close connections with other girls, even if they were just friends. It was a complex dance of jealousy and uncertainty, revealing a side of Akshi that she hadn't anticipated.

Making Memories

"Memories are timeless treasures of the heart."

Memories are more than just moments in time. They are precious treasures that we carry with us throughout our lives, and they hold a special place in our hearts.

Everything was going smoothly between Paras and Akshi; they had become the best of friends. They talked to each other every day, and their bond was growing stronger with each passing day. They became inseparable, talking daily, and their bond strengthened with each passing moment. However, within the harmonious melody of their friendship, a subtle dissonance played in the background of Akshi's mind. The awareness that Paras had a best friend, Myra, whom she had never met, created a whisper of unease. Weekend came, Paras and Myra decided to visit the art gallery after a long time. They spent the day exploring the art gallery, laughing over coffee, and creating memories. Myra, capturing the essence of their day, posted a cheerful Instagram story featuring Paras and herself at the art gallery.

Akshi, saw a vibrant photo on Instagram as Paras reposted Myra's story, featuring himself and Myra, both smiling radiantly in front of a captivating piece of art. The caption read, "Reunited with this bundle of joy after ages. A day well spent with my forever friend, Myra!

Intrigued, she decided to reach out to Myra. She sent a friendly direct message with a follow. She notices the genuine happiness captured in the photo. Curious, she decided to reply to Paras's story, "Looks like an amazing day! Who's the bundle of joy, though?"

Paras, always enthusiastic about sharing his world with Akshi, replied, "Meet Myra, my partner-in-crime. We once met at an art gallery, and became best of friends as time passed and after a long time we reunited. I told you that day when she called in front of you. You should join us sometime!"

Akshi suppressing her jealousy, "Ohh! Best friends, yeah yeah you told me before. I also wanted a best friend in my life. Why not, I'll surely join you guys some time. Let me add her on Instagram in the meantime."

The conversation between Akshi and Myra flourished naturally. They talked about poetry, art, and, of course, Paras. Akshi felt a hint of insecurity creeping in as Myra shared stories of their long-lasting friendship. The mere mention of Paras brought forth a flood of questions in Akshi's mind.

Akshi typing nervously, So, how long have you known Paras?

Myra, Oh! Paras and I go way back. We met in an art gallery and have been best friends ever since. He's an amazing person, you know.

Akshi trying to sound casual, Yeah, he is. It's just that we've been spending a lot of time together recently.

Myra cheerfully, That's fantastic! Paras always talks about you; he never gets tired of sharing you hangout stories. I'm glad you guys are together.

Akshi and Myra became friends on social media. As they grew closer, Myra shared memories of her and Paras before Akshi came into his life, leaving Akshi feel somewhat insecure about their bond. At home, alone with her thoughts, Akshi hesitated before texting Paras. "Hey Paras, Myra's really cool. I'm glad we're friends. But sometimes, I feel like there's this whole world of memories and experiences I'm not a part of. Is that strange?"

Paras, quick to respond, replied, "Not at all, Akshi. Myra's an old friend, and you're my present. We're creating our own world, one day at a time. And she's just my best friend nothing else."

Akshi smiled at the message, comforted yet aware that navigating the complexities of their friendships required a delicate balance. Amid Paras and Akshi's blossoming friendship, there was another significant relationship in Paras's life: his bond with Myra. She often joked that she was Paras's "relationship consultant," offering insights and perspectives on matters of the heart. Paras, in turn, was Myra's go-to person for anything and everything. Their bond went beyond the superficial; it was a connection of shared laughter, shared tears, and a shared understanding that true friendship knows no bounds. As Paras was on a video call with Myra and talking about how much he enjoyed spending time with Akshi, he suddenly received a text from her.

He grinned and showed the message to Myra. "Hey, it's Akshi! She's inviting me to her house today. Her parents are out of town, and she's feeling a bit lonely. She wants us to hang out and cook something together," Paras said excitedly.

Myra, with her usual sarcastic tone, teased, "Oh, wow, Mr. Popular! Invited to a private hangout at Akshi's house, huh? Don't forget your chef hat!"

Paras rolled his eyes playfully. "It's nothing like that, Myra. We're just friends, and she said she wanted to try cooking Dal Makhani and Rotis together."

Myra chuckled. "Of course, "just friends" But you know, sometimes cooking together can lead to something more, like a recipe for love!"

Paras laughed, "You and your wild imagination! It's not like that at all. Akshi and I are just enjoying each other's company you know."

Myra smiled knowingly. "Well, who knows what the future holds? Maybe this cooking session will be a turning point for you both. But in the meantime, have fun, Chef Paras!"

With a smirk, Paras replied, "Thanks, Myra. I'll see you later. And stop teasing me!"

As he arrived at Akshi's home, he found her waiting at the

door with a warm smile. "Hey, come on in! I've been looking forward to this cooking session all day.

They started assembling items to make dal makhani, and rotis and started cooking, with Paras taking the lead in making the rotis. To Akshi's surprise, he had an impressive technique, perfectly rolling out the dough and cooking the rotis on the hot skillet. Akshi admires Paras's skills in the kitchen. He was a natural, making perfect rotis and chopping vegetables with ease.

Akshi, on the other hand, was struggling with the spices, often forgetting which ones to use and in what order. But Paras was patient and guided her through each step, making sure the food turned out delicious.

"Wow, Paras! You're a natural at making rotis!" Akshi said in amazement.

Paras grinned. "I may not be a pro, but I know my way around the kitchen. My mom used to make me help her out in the kitchen when I was younger."

As they continued cooking, a little flour got spilt on the kitchen counter, and Akshi jokingly tossed a small amount of flour at Paras, which started a playful dough fight between the two.

Paras took a handful of flour and threw it at Akshi, hitting her lightly on the cheek. Akshi retaliated by throwing a handful of dough at Paras, which stuck to his shirt. They both burst out laughing, their playfulness turning into a full-on dough fight. Soon, the kitchen was covered in flour, and they were both covered in dough. They collapsed onto the couch, out of breath from all the laughing and playfulness. After the dough fight, Paras and Akshi finally got to work and started making the rotis.

"This was so much fun, Akshi. We should do this more often," Paras said, grinning from ear to ear.

Akshi smiled back. "Definitely! It's been a while since I had so much fun in the kitchen. You know, I was a bit scared before you came.

There was a theft incident in our society, and I was home alone."

Paras looked surprised. "What? Why didn't you tell me earlier? Are you okay?"

Akshi nodded. "Yeah, I'm fine now. I was just a bit scared earlier. But having you here made me feel better."

Paras looked relieved. "I'm glad I could be here for you, Akshi. You know, I had a great time today. You're an amazing cook and a great friend."

Akshi smiled, feeling grateful for having Paras. "Thanks, Paras. You're pretty amazing yourself."

The aroma of the delicious meal lingered in the air as Paras and Akshi sat down to savour the fruits of their culinary efforts. The table was adorned with an array of colourful dishes, a testament to their collaborative cooking adventure. The soft glow of candles flickered, casting a warm ambience that added to the coziness of the room. The clinking of cutlery against plates accompanied the pleasant symphony of their laughter and conversation.

It was a scene painted with the hues of friendship and shared moments. As they delved into their meal, the conversation flowed effortlessly. Paras marvels at the depth and breadth of Akshi's experiences. She spoke passionately about her journey through the world of finance and the various volunteer organizations she dedicated her time to. Her eyes sparkled with enthusiasm as she shared stories of the lives she had touched through her financial advice and the community work she was involved in. Paras, in turn, opened up about his aspirations and dreams. The discussion shifted seamlessly from their academic pursuits to their post-graduation plans. Akshi expressed her admiration for Paras's ambition and drive. She found his choice of pursuing an MBA intriguing and exciting, and Paras reciprocated the sentiment. They spoke about the business schools they aspired to attend, sharing anecdotes about the rigorous admission processes and the challenges they anticipated. Paras was drawn to Akshi's intellect and her ability to navigate the complexities of the financial world, and Akshi found in Paras a kindred spirit with a shared passion for personal and professional growth. As they indulged in the delicious meal, their connection deepened. Each bite seemed to symbolize not just the flavours of the food but also the richness of the bond they were building.

Para said "I was thinking... what if we went to the same college for our MBA?" he asked uneasily, staring at Akshi.

In disbelief, Akshi's eyes widened.

"Really?" she asked. "I was thinking the same thing."

As the laughter and chatter filled the air, Paras and Akshi exchanged smiles that carried the unspoken acknowledgement of the growing bond between them. The warmth of their shared experiences and dreams lingered in the room as they continued to enjoy the remnants of their delightful meal. Amidst the relaxed atmosphere, he ringing of Akshi's phone momentarily stirred the calm surroundings. With a polite apology, she excused herself to take the call, her face lighting up as she recognized her mother's number flashing on the screen. A quick exchange of greetings and the mention of her parents being on their way home prompted Akshi to conclude the call with a promise to see them shortly. The realization that their cosy evening was coming to an end prompted a swift transition into action.

Akshi, now wearing a gentle smile, conveyed the news to Paras, and they both began to gather the remnants of their culinary adventure.

While cleaning up, Paras couldn't resist teasing Akshi. "You're not as good at cleaning up as you are at cooking," he joked.

Akshi rolled her eyes. "Oh, please. You're just saying that because you don't want to do any work."

Paras laughed. "You got me there. But I have to say, you did make some great food."

Akshi smiled. "Thanks. You were a great sous chef too. And your rotis were perfect."

Paras beamed with pride. "I learned from the best."

As they finished cleaning up, Akshi turned to Paras and gave him a warm hug.

"Thank you for being here with me today, Paras. It was nice to have your company."

Paras hugged her back and replied, "Anytime, Akshi. I had a great time too."

As they pulled away from the hug, Akshi looked at Paras and said, "You know, I was really scared when I called you over earlier. But you made me feel safe and comfortable. Thank you for being there for me."

Paras smiled and placed a hand on her shoulder. "Of course, Akshi. I'm always here for you if you need me."

Akshi smiled back at him, feeling grateful to have such a supportive friend in her life. They said their goodbyes as Akshi's parents walked in the door, and Paras left with a happy feeling in his heart.

As Paras lay in bed that night, his mind was filled with thoughts of Akshi. In the quiet solitude of his room, the soft glow of the bedside lamp casting a warm ambience, Paras found himself wrestling with a swirl of conflicting emotions. The laughter and shared moments with Akshi lingered in his mind, but so did the echoes of past heartbreaks. As he lay in bed, a sense of weekness washed over him, prompting an internal dialogue that sought to navigate the intricate landscape of his emotions. His thoughts, like threads weaving through the fabric of his consciousness, wove a tapestry of uncertainty and longing. The connection with Akshi felt undeniable, a magnetic pull that transcended the boundaries of ordinary friendships. Yet, beneath the surface, the scars of previous heartaches lay dormant, acting as cautious sentinels guarding the gates of his emotions.

Paras, in a silent conversation with himself, adopted a tone of self-reflection, as though trying to reason with the most vulnerable corners of his heart. The words were a gentle reminder, a cautionary tale spoken to the depths of his soul.

"Look," he began, his internal voice carrying a weight of experience, "I know you feel something for Akshi. The laughter, the connection, it's undeniable. But you can't forget what you've been through. The pain, the heartache it's etched in your memories. You can't afford to let yourself get too involved and risk going through that again." The timbre of his inner voice revealed a helplessness, a hesitancy born out of the scars of the past. Paras grappled with the fear of attachment, the worry that investing too much of himself might lead to another chapter of heartbreak. The spectre of his previous relationship cast a long shadow, influencing his current perceptions and decisions.

He continued the internal conversation, the sincerity in his tone reflecting the genuine conflict within. "It's not that you don't want to be close to Akshi. It's just... you've been hurt before. And it's okay to be cautious. You need to protect yourself and guard your heart. Don't let the allure of the present cloud your judgment about the potential risks."

His inner voice agreed, but it also reminded him of how much joy Akshi had brought into his life. "Yes, you have to be cautious, but you also can't shut yourself off from the possibility of happiness. Akshi seems like a wonderful person, and your connection with her is undeniable. Don't let the fear of getting hurt hold you back from something beautiful."

The soft glow of dawn painted the room in hues of warmth as Paras, in the stillness of the morning, revisited the conversation with his inner voice. The conflicting thoughts echoed in his mind, a delicate dance between caution and the allure of newfound happiness. His inner voice, a gentle yet persistent companion, reminded him of the joy that Akshi had brought into his life. "Yes, you have to be cautious," it whispered, "but you also can't shut yourself off from the possibility of happiness. Akshi seems like a wonderful person, and your connection with her is undeniable. Don't let the fear of getting hurt hold you back from something beautiful."

Paras mulled over these opposing sentiments, his thoughts a canvas painted with shades of vulnerability and hope. He didn't want the shackles of his past to restrain him from the potential of a meaningful relationship. Akshi, with her infectious laughter and genuine spirit, had become a source of joy in his life a bright spot in the tapestry of his days. As the morning sun bathed the room, Paras grappled with the scars that lingered within him. The wounds of past heartbreaks had, at times, spoken louder than the whispers of newfound connection. But, amidst the tangle of conflicting emotions, a realization began to take root. He acknowledged that unexpected things often led to the most enjoyable experiences. Akshi had become more than a friend; she was a beacon of warmth in his life. Paras felt thankful for the unexpected twist of fate that had brought them together, transcending the boundaries of casual acquaintanceship.

The next day brought with it a message from Akshi, a simple yet heartfelt thank you for the camaraderie shared the previous night. Paras, with a smile playing on his lips, replied in kind. He expressed not only the fun he had experienced but also the genuine happiness of having made a new connection. Akshi leaned against the railing of the balcony, the soft glow of the setting sun casting a warm hue over her features. She glanced down at her phone, her heart fluttering as she composed a message to Paras.

"Hey, Paras. I wanted to thank you for yesterday. It meant a lot to me," she typed, her fingers tapping lightly on the screen.

A faint smile tugged at Paras's lips as he read her message. He quickly composed a reply, feeling a sense of contentment wash over him. "Akshi! No need to thank me. I had a great time too," he responded.

Akshi's heart skipped a beat as she read his reply. She took a deep breath and continued typing, her gratitude spilling into her words. "Seriously, though. Your honesty and openness meant a lot. I appreciate it," she confessed, her gratitude shining through.

He replied, his admiration evident in his words. "Well, I believe in being real. You are important to me."

Akshi, her gaze softened "Mine too. It's been a while since I connected with someone like this."

Paras, nodding in agreement "Same here. You make talking about even serious stuff seem easy."

Akshi, with a playful glint in her eyes "Haha, well, that's one of my superpowers."

Paras, chuckling "Clearly!"

Akshi, teasingly "Thanks again, Paras. Looking forward to more chats... and maybe some fun MBA plans."

Paras, with a mischievous grin "Absolutely! MBA power duo in the making."

Akshi, sharing the laughter "You got it! Hahaha"

Paras, transitioning to a more serious topic "Btw, what are your plans for your MBA studies?"

Akshi, thoughtful "I'm still thinking about it, but I'm leaning towards marketing or finance. So, how about you?"

Paras, contemplating "I'm considering operations management or entrepreneurship. I've always wanted to launch my own business."

Akshi, intrigued "That's great. What kind of company do you want to start?"

Paras, a gleam in his eyes "I'm not sure yet, perhaps

something in the clothing business, like a clothing brand. So, how about you? Have you considered what you want to do after graduation?"

Akshi, with a dreamy expression "I've always wanted to work for a large firm, either in the fashion or beauty industries. But I also want to open my own business, like a boutique or an online store, someday."

Paras, appreciating her ambitions "That's fantastic! I could easily picture you running your own company. You have excellent taste and a strong sense of style."

Akshi, blushing slightly "Thanks, Paras. What about you? Do you think you'll start your own business right after graduation?"

Paras, with a contemplative expression "I'm not sure. I think I'll probably gain some experience working for a big company first, and then maybe start my own thing down the line. But who knows? Anything could happen."

Akshi, smiling "Yeah, that's true. I'm excited to see where life takes us after college."

Paras, sharing her excitement "Me too. And who knows? Maybe we'll even end up working together someday. Btw If you're free right now let's have an evening walk together"

Akshi, laughing "That would be cool. But we'll have to see where our paths take us first. Yeah sure coming in 10 min"

They both met at a meeting point and strolled towards Paras's favourite park, where a serene lake awaited to be painted in the hues of the setting sun. The atmosphere was infused with a gentle breeze, carrying the fragrance of blooming flowers. As they entered the park, Paras felt a sense of déjà vu. He glanced around, and it struck him that he had seen Akshi here before. It was a memory tucked away, a scene from his past when he was walking down the street with his friend. Akshi was playing with a little puppy, her laughter echoing in the air. What intrigued him even more was that she was wearing the same dress as that day. A subtle realization washed over him, but Paras decided to keep this revelation to himself. He didn't want to make the situation awkward, and instead, he chose to cherish the present moment.

Paras "She looks so beautiful, so at peace. This feels like a dream. Akshi, bathed in the warm hues of the sunset, looks like an enchanting painting. The way her hair catches the last rays of sunlight, and the glow on her face it's mesmerizing. But hold on, I've seen this before, haven't I? That day with my friend, the park, the puppy... and she's wearing that same dress. What are the odds? Yet, should I mention it? No, not now. it might make things awkward. Let's just enjoy this moment.

They found a quiet corner bench overlooking the lake and settled down. The sky was a canvas of warm hues, reflecting on the tranquil water. The sun descended gracefully, casting a golden glow across the landscape. Paras initiated a conversation, steering it away from the odd connection he felt. The warmth of their words blended seamlessly with the fading sunlight.

Paras, a subtle smile playing on his lips, expressed, "Akshi, amidst the canvas of the evening sky, you're the most beautiful stroke of color. I can't help but feel a connection with this place, a déjà vu, as if fate conspired to bring us back here."

Akshi, her cheeks tinged with a blush, responded, "You're sweet, Paras. I never thought a park could feel so magical."

Paras, gazing into her eyes with a genuine warmth, confessed, "It's not just the park; it's the company. You bring a certain magic wherever you go."

Internally debating whether to share a significant memory, Paras decided against it, opting to let the present moment be solely about them.

Still smiling, Paras continued, "Akshi, have you ever felt like you've known someone forever, even if you just met?"

Akshi, thoughtful, replied, "Yeah, I have. It's like an instant connection, right?"

Paras nodded, adding, "Exactly. Sometimes, places hold memories, and sometimes, they create new ones."

As the sun dipped below the horizon, painting the sky in shades of orange and pink, Paras appreciated the beauty of the moment. The memory of Akshi playing with the puppy in the same park was now a subtle thread connecting their past and present.

Paras, smiling warmly, remarked, "So, what's your favorite thing about sunsets?"

Akshi, her expression thoughtful, responded, "I think it's the calm that descends, the feeling that the world is slowing down for a moment. And, of course, the colors they're so magical."

Paras, nodding in agreement, added, "I completely agree. It's like nature's way of saying, 'Pause and appreciate.'"

The two sat there, enveloped in the calmness of the evening, sharing stories and laughter until the last light disappeared.

Akshi, a genuine smile on her face, said, "Paras, you know what, I'm really grateful for our friendship. It means a lot to me. We make great friends, don't we?"

Paras, though his smile remained, there was a hint of something beneath the surface, forcing a smile as he replied, "Yeah, great friends." His forced smile betrayed a complexity of emotions, suggesting that there might be more to the story than what his words conveyed.

He began to develop feelings for Akshi but wasn't sure she's thinking the same. They shared so many moments together but its like she's keeping him in friendzone even sharing intimate moments together.

Paras, his thoughts a whirlwind of emotions, pondered internally, "Friendship, again. Why does she keep emphasizing it? We're sitting here, sharing this beautiful moment, and yet, it's like she's drawing a line. Does she not feel what I'm feeling?"

The frustration lingered in Paras's heart, a silent storm amidst the serenity of the park. He wanted to express more, to move beyond the confines of friendship, but the fear of disrupting the delicate balance held him back. As they strolled side by side, Paras felt a mixture of gratitude for the chance encounter and an undercurrent of frustration. The emphasis on the word "friends" echoed in his mind, a constant reminder of a boundary he yearned to cross.

Akshi, her tone casual yet filled with warmth, said, "I'm really glad we're friends again after school, it means a lot."

Internally, Paras felt a whirlwind of conflicting emotions. "Friends, friends, friends. Why does she keep saying that? We just shared a beautiful evening, a connection. Is she oblivious to what's developing between us? Do I tell her now what I'm feeling?"

Akshi, grinning with genuine joy, added, "Paras, this was so much fun! We should do it again sometime, as best friends do."

Paras, though he forced a smile, couldn't shake off the internal turmoil. "Yeah, friends. Absolutely." His mind raced, contemplating the delicate balance between preserving a connection and the fear of losing something more profound.

Internally, he coached himself, "No, Paras, no. What if you lose this beautiful connection with her? You don't want to lose her. Calm down!" The dance between their words and unspoken sentiments created a poignant atmosphere, hanging in the space between friendship and the unexplored realms of something deeper.

Paras couldn't shake off the twinge of frustration that had been building within him. As they walked under the city lights, He spotted his sister, Sachi, standing at a nearby intersection, engrossed in a conversation with a friend. His heart skipped a beat, realization hitting him that Sachi might have seen him with Akshi.

Panic flickered in Paras' eyes, and his mind raced to devise a quick plan. Turning to Akshi with a hurried smile, he said, "Hey, change of plans. Let's take a different route home, avoid the crowd a bit."

Akshi, blissfully unaware of the reason behind the sudden shift, agreed with a smile, and they swiftly altered their course. As they walked, Paras couldn't shake off the nervous energy, periodically glancing over his shoulder to ensure they weren't being followed. Akshi, sensing his unease but clueless about the cause, attempted to lighten the mood with casual conversation.

Paras, breaking the usual route, expressed, "Hey, thanks for being cool about changing our route back there. I just felt like taking a quieter way."

Akshi, easygoing, responded, "No problem at all! But I'm curious, why the sudden change?"

Paras, a hint of nervousness in his voice, replied, "Oh, just thought it would be a bit more peaceful. You know, crowds and all."

Akshi, sensing something more, inquired, "Fair enough. You seemed a bit in a hurry, though. Is everything okay?"

Paras, attempting to deflect, hastily added, "Yeah, yeah, all good. Just realized we could avoid some traffic. So, what's new with you?"

Akshi, raising an eyebrow, pressed on, "Not much, just the usual. But you're acting a bit strange. Anything you're not telling me?"

Paras, hesitating, finally admitted, "Nah, suddenly just had a lot on my mind. Work, studies, you know how it is."

Akshi, concerned, reassured, "If you say so. But you know you can talk to me, right?"

Paras, appreciative, replied, "I appreciate that, Akshi. Just some personal stuff, nothing to worry about."

Akshi, still a bit confused, said, "Alright, if you say so." The air carried a subtle tension, leaving a lingering feeling that there might be more beneath the surface of Paras' casual explanation.

Paras, however, was preoccupied with thoughts of his sister spotting them together. He guided Akshi out of the crowded area, leaving in a hurry without explaining the sudden change. Akshi, left slightly puzzled, her overthinking tendencies kicked in. She began to wonder if there was something more to the situation, inadvertently adding a layer of complexity to their seemingly casual outing. The abrupt alteration in plans planted seeds of curiosity and speculation in Akshi's mind as they continued their walk in a different direction, leaving the air charged with unspoken questions. As Paras reached home, Sachi was sitting in the living room, engrossed in her phone. She looked up as Paras entered, a sly grin on her face. "Well, well, look who's home. Who was that girl you were with?"

Paras rolled his eyes, "Come on, Sachi, don't start."

Sachi teased, "Oh, is she your new friend? Or something more?"

Paras sighed, knowing his sister too well. "She's just a friend, Sachi, her name is Akshi. We bumped into each other, and we decided to grab a coffee. That's it."

Sachi raised an eyebrow, "Just a friend, huh? Well, I hope you're not hiding anything. You know I can find out.

Paras chuckled, "You're not a detective, Sachi. And there's nothing to hide. We're just friends, getting to know each other."

Sachi shrugged, "Alright, don't say I didn't warn you. But if she's just a friend, why did you change your route?"

Paras hesitated for a moment, then grinned, "Just felt like taking a scenic route, you know me."

Sachi laughed, not entirely convinced, but dropped the subject. "Alright, Mr. Mysterious. Just remember, I'm watching."

As Paras retreated to his room, he reflected on how much he valued his sister's nosy yet caring nature. Little did he know that Sachi would keep a watchful eye on his budding friendship with Akshi, ready to play the role of the protective sibling. As he was chilling sitting on his bed reading the uncompleted novel Sachi entered and asked about Akshi.

"So, Paras, tell me more about this 'just friends' thing with Akshi. She seems nice," Sachi said with a mischievous grin.

Paras chuckled, "We are just friends, Sachi. But who knows

what the future holds?"

Sachi nodded with a knowing smile, "Fair enough. Just remember, I've got my eyes on you two!"

Paras rolled his eyes playfully, "Don't worry, Sachi. I'll keep you in the loop."

And with that, he continued reading the novel. Paras felt grateful for his sister's approval and excited about the budding friendship he had with Akshi but as they were sitting in the same room, Sachi adopted a more serious tone. "You know, Paras, I've seen many girls play with boys' feelings. Be careful, okay? I don't want to see you get hurt."

Paras appreciated his sister's concern and replied, "I know, Sachi. I'm not looking to rush into anything. Akshi and I are just getting to know each other as friends, and that's all it is for now. I don't even feel for her in that sense as of now."

Sachi nodded approvingly. "Good. Focus on your career, your goals and mainly on your MBA. Relationships can wait. You have a bright future ahead, and I don't want anything to distract you from that."

"I promise, Sachi. My career comes first," Paras assured her.

Sachi smiled and put her arm around her brother's shoulder. "That's my boy. I know you'll make us all proud. Just take things slow, and if something more develops with Akshi, just be sure to communicate openly with each other."

"I will, Sachi. Thanks for looking out for me," Paras replied gratefully.

Sachi squeezed his shoulder affectionately. "You're welcome. You know I'll always be here for you, right? No matter what."

Paras smiled, feeling grateful for his sister's unwavering support. "I know, Sachi. And I'm lucky to have you as my sister."

On the other hand, Akshi replayed the events of the day in her mind. The sudden change in route after Paras spotted his sister had left her feeling a bit perplexed. She liked Paras; he was a great guy, and their friendship was blossoming. But the abrupt shift in their walk had triggered her overthinking tendencies.

As she entered her apartment, her mind was a whirlwind of questions.

Why did he change the route so suddenly? Did he see someone he didn't want to run into? Her analytical mind was working overtime. The casual conversation they shared during the walk couldn't distract her from the lingering uncertainty.

That evening, as she sat in her living room, a message from Paras popped up on her phone.

"Hey, sorry about changing the route earlier. My sister was around, and I didn't want to get into a long conversation. I hope you understand."

Akshi read the message, her eyebrows furrowing with curiosity. His sister? The sudden change seemed more than just avoiding a conversation. She couldn't shake the feeling that there might be more to the story. Tentatively, she replied.

Akshi No problem at all! Thanks for letting me know. Is everything okay with your sister? We can always take the scenic route next time.

Paras Definitely! Looking forward to it.

The exchange left Akshi with a mix of relief and a lingering sense of curiosity. She couldn't help but wonder if there was more to the story than Paras let on. As the days turned into weeks, Paras and Akshi's friendship deepened but that incident still bothers Akshi. She always thought if his sister was there why he didn't introduce her to his sister. On the other hand, Paras notices how comfortable and happy he feels when he is with Akshi. She was like a breath of fresh air in his life, bringing joy and positivity into every moment they spent together. He admired her ambition, her kind heart, and her ability to see the beauty in the smallest of things. One evening, as they were sitting on a park bench, watching the sunset, Akshi leaned onto Paras's shoulder, he felt a warmth in his heart that he hadn't experienced in a long time. He realized that he was now building feelings for Akshi beyond just friendship. He couldn't deny the attraction he felt towards her, and it scared him a little. He knew he had to be cautious. After all, he had been through a painful breakup in the past, and he didn't want to rush into anything without being sure of his emotions. He decided to ignore that feeling and cherish their friendship, giving himself time to truly understand what he felt for Akshi. He wanted to tell Akshi about his feelings, but he was also afraid of jeopardizing their beautiful friendship. He feared that confessing his emotions might change their dynamic, and he didn't want to risk losing the bond they had built. One evening, as they were sitting on the rooftop, watching the sunset, Paras felt a mix of happiness and sadness. He wanted to tell Akshi about his feelings, to let her know how much she meant to him, but he held himself back.

"Akshi," Paras started, his voice slightly trembling, "I want you to know that you're one of the most special people in my life. Our friendship means the world to me, and I cherish every moment we spend together."

Akshi smiled warmly at him, her eyes shining with affection. "You're one of my closest friends too, Paras. I'm grateful for our bond and the way we can be ourselves around each other."

Paras took a deep breath, trying to find the right words, but he hesitated. He couldn't bring himself to reveal his true feelings, afraid of the potential consequences. Akshi sensed his unease and gently placed her hand on his. "Is there something else you want to say, Paras?"

Paras looked into her eyes, feeling a swirl of emotions inside him. He wanted to tell her, but the fear of rejection held him back. "No, it's nothing. I'm just glad to have you in my life."

Akshi smiled softly, giving his hand a reassuring squeeze. "Me too, Paras. You're an amazing friend, and I value our connection more than words can express." As they sat in comfortable silence, Paras felt a mix of relief and regret. He knew he had chosen not to reveal his feelings, but he also knew that he had made the right decision for now. He wanted to preserve their friendship and take things slow, giving himself time to truly understand his emotions.

"Sometimes, the most beautiful and meaningful relationships are those where words remain unspoken, and emotions dance in the silence."

Falling into you

"Love is not a noun to be defined, but a verb to be acted upon."

Love is not just a feeling or an idea that can be neatly defined and put into a box. Instead, love is an active force that requires action and effort to truly be felt and experienced. To truly fall in love with someone, we must not only feel love for them but also actively show them that love through our actions. This could mean doing kind things for them, making sacrifices to help them, or simply spending quality time with them.

His heart becoming a canvas painted with the vivid hues of affection and yearning. What began as a simple friendship had morphed into a complex tapestry of feelings, each interaction with Akshi weaving a new thread into the fabric of his emotions.

The platonic bond, once defined by laughter and shared interests, now resonated with a profound resonance that tugged at Paras' understanding. It was as if an enchanting spell had been cast, enveloping him in a warmth that transcended the boundaries of friendship. Paras, usually composed and level-headed, discovered himself adrift in the unpredictable currents of emotions. Thoughts of Akshi became a constant companion, a pleasant intrusion in his daily life. The echo of her laughter, the gleam in her eyes, and the vibrant energy she infused into his existence lingered in his mind long after their conversations ended. The prospect of their upcoming meet-ups became a source of delightful anticipation, a fluttering in his heart that betrayed the calm exterior he usually wore. Paras, ever the rational thinker, found himself grappling to understand this emotional metamorphosis. The magnetic pull towards Akshi was undeniable, an invisible force that drew him closer with each passing day. His friends, especially Myra, keen observers of his changing demeanor, couldn't help but notice the shift. Myra, his trusted close friend, playfully teased him about being lovestruck, yet Paras, fearing the potential consequences of admitting his feelings, dismissed it with a nervous laugh. The reality was evident, though Paras was falling, and he was falling hard. The simple moments shared with Akshi became precious fragments of his daily life.

Myra, teasingly, remarked, "Hey lovestruck, what's with the dreamy look these days?"

Paras, attempting to play it cool, replied, "Dreamy look? I have no idea what you're talking about."

Myra, with a knowing smile, insisted, "Please, I've known you forever. Something's definitely up. Tell me!"

Paras, giving in to her persistence, admitted, "Alright, alright.

Maybe there's a slight shift in the universe, but it's nothing major."

Myra, adopting a playful tone, teased, "A 'slight shift in the universe'? Seriously, Paras? Is this your attempt at downplaying the fact that you're head over heels?"

Paras, nervously laughing, responded, "Come on, Myra, don't exaggerate. We're just good friends, you know."

Myra, with a touch of sarcasm, said, "Oh, of course, just friends. The kind of friends who can't stop thinking about each other, right?"

Myra: Messy or not, it's written all over your face. You're falling hard, my friend.

Paras, acknowledging the truth, conceded, "Okay, maybe there's a bit more to it. But you know how messy things can get when feelings are involved."

Paras, a hint of uncertainty in his voice, sighed, "Yeah, I can't deny that. But what if it complicates everything? What if I ruin what we have?"

Myra, with a reassuring smile, replied, "Fear of the unknown, my dear. But you won't know unless you take a chance. Besides, a little messiness is what makes life interesting."

Paras, lost in thought, mused, "You might have a point there." Myra, advised, "Trust me, it's better to try and stumble than to spend your days wondering 'what if.'"

In the quiet corners of his thoughts, Paras admitted to himself that something had changed. The infectious quality of Akshi's laughter, the way she casually tossed her hair, and the subtle crinkle in her eyes when she smiled became precious details etched into his memory. Paras marveled at how Akshi had seamlessly become a source of joy, injecting vitality into the otherwise mundane patterns of his daily existence. Little did he realize that these simple fragments were painting a canvas of emotions that went beyond the boundaries of mere friendship. As night fell, and Paras lay in bed staring at the ceiling, his thoughts spiraled into contemplation. The realization that he had fallen for Akshi struck him like a bolt of lightning again. The longing to express his emotions tugged at his heartstrings, but fear gripped him. He grappled with the dilemma of wanting to confess his feelings and the apprehension of jeopardizing the beautiful connection they had cultivated. Patience, he reasoned with himself. The need to let their relationship evolve organically echoed in his mind. Yet, the intensity of his emotions made this a challenging feat. Paras was caught in a whirlwind of emotions, a storm of love, uncertainty, and anticipation. He recognized that he had traversed into uncharted territory, head over heels in love with Akshi, and there was no turning back. The weight of unspoken words lingered, leaving Paras in a state of both blissful euphoria and cautious anxiety.

In the delicate dance between past scars and budding affections, Akshi found herself in a delicate balancing act, standing at the crossroads of vulnerability and caution. Her heart carried the weight of past tumults, a collection of scars that painted her approach to romance with hues of hesitancy. Each step forward seemed shadowed by the ghosts of heartbreaks, leaving her grappling with the question of whether she was truly ready to open herself to the possibility of new love. Paras, oblivious to the depth of Akshi's internal struggles, was resolute in his quest to win her heart. Every gesture, every action was meticulously crafted to make her feel cherished and understood. His unwavering attentiveness, coupled with genuine compassion, created an ambiance of comfort and security around Akshi. Paras was not merely a friend; he was a companion, a confidant, and a pillar of support. Yet, despite Paras's earnest efforts, Akshi remained hesitant. The echoes of past heartbreaks reverberated in her mind, creating a hesitancy to embrace the possibility of love once more. Paras's admission of his feelings, an expression of genuine affection, added a layer of complexity to their relationship.

Paras, with a hint of nervousness, approached Akshi, "Akshi, can I talk to you about something?"

Akshi looked at him curiously. "Of course, Paras. You know you can talk to me about anything."

Paras took a deep breath, his heart pounding in his chest. "I... I can't help but feel that my feelings for you have grown beyond just friendship. You mean so much to me, and I can't deny the connection we have. I think I'm falling for you, Akshi."

Akshi's eyes widened with surprise, and for a moment, she seemed at a loss for words. "Paras, I... I don't know what to say. You've made this complicated now, and I value our friendship too. You're an incredible person. But I've been hurt in the past, and I'm scared of getting into something I'm not ready for."

Paras nodded understandingly, trying to hide his disappointment. "I understand, Akshi. I don't want to pressure you or make things awkward between us."

Akshi smiled gratefully at him, relieved that he wasn't pushing her. "Thank you, Paras. You're so understanding, and I don't want to lose our friendship either."

When confronted with Paras's heartfelt revelation, Akshi found herself caught in a web of conflicting emotions. The familiarity of uncertainty danced with the desire for something profound and genuine. Rather than confront her own ambiguity, Akshi, grappling with a tumult of emotions, labeled their relationship as "Complicated." This label, though succinct, became a shield that Akshi wielded to navigate the intricate landscape of her emotions. It became a placeholder for the unspoken fears, the wariness of potential heartbreak, and the struggle to reconcile past wounds with the burgeoning feelings in the present. Later, with confusion swirling in his mind, Paras asked Akshi, "What did you mean by 'complicated'? I know we've spent a lot of time together recently, and I think there's something more between us."

Akshi sighed, "As I said, you're a fantastic person, Paras, and I love spending time with you. But I recently got out of a difficult relationship, and I'm not sure I'm ready to start over."

Paras, with a slightly slowed voice, replied, "I understand, but I just wanted to let you know that I care about you and am prepared to take things slowly. I don't want to lose you."

Akshi expressed her gratitude, "I appreciate that, but I need some time to think things through. Can we just be friends for the time being?"

"Of course," Paras replied with a tinge of sadness in his heart, trying to remain calm in front of Akshi. "Just know that I'm always here for you." Paras couldn't comprehend the sudden distance that had emerged between him and Akshi. The warmth that once defined their interactions now seemed replaced by an unspoken tension; a subtle shift that left Paras bewildered. His unwavering determination to nurture their connection had hit an unexpected roadblock as Akshi began to weave a tapestry of evasive maneuvers. Every attempt to spend time with her was met with dodges and excuses, that left Paras disheartened. Despite the growing chasm, Paras persisted in reaching out, hoping to bridge the widening gap. However, Akshi's responses became increasingly elusive, leaving Paras feeling like an actor on a stage, performing a role in a play whose script he hadn't been given. It was as though a curtain had fallen between them, obscuring the once clear lines of communication.

Paras grappled with the uncertainty of Akshi's feelings, unsure whether the distance was a consequence of external factors or an intentional effort to create space. The warmth that once enveloped their friendship now seemed replaced by a chill, and Paras navigating the complex dynamics of a relationship whose script had taken an unforeseen turn. For Akshi, the act of dodging was a self-preserving defense mechanism, a way to grapple with the inner turmoil she found herself entangled in. The complexity of her emotions, coupled with the haunting shadows of past heartaches, became a formidable barrier that she wasn't ready to dismantle. The dance of avoidance, though painful for Paras, became a shield for Akshi as she navigated the intricate web of her own feelings. As days turned into weeks, the shift in dynamics between Paras and Akshi became increasingly intense. The once vibrant bond of their friendship now bore the unmistakable marks of tension and distance. Paras, who had bared his soul in a vulnerable admission of his feelings, found himself traversing the uncertain terrain of Akshi's newfound reluctance. The "complicated" label hung between them like a delicate thread, connecting them yet keeping them at a cautious distance. Paras, ever attuned to the nuances of their interactions, couldn't escape the subtle signs of Akshi's withdrawal. Their usual hangouts, once characterized by laughter and shared moments, became rarer as she began weaving a tapestry of excuses to avoid them. The warmth that had once defined their connection now seemed replaced by a cool breeze of uncertainty, leaving Paras caught in a whirlwind of emotions he struggled to comprehend.

(Several days later)

Concerned, Paras reached out, "Hey, I haven't heard from you in a long time. Is everything all right?"

Akshi, conveying busyness and distraction, replied, "Oh, I'm sorry about that. I've just been preoccupied with college work and household."

Paras, trying to bridge the gap, suggested, "That's very understandable. I was thinking about meeting you for dinner tonight if you're available."

Akshi, burdened with tasks, responded, "I have a lot of work to do, Paras. Maybe another time?"

Paras, acknowledging the situation, reassured, "Yeah, no problem. Just let me know when you're free."

Akshi, appreciating the understanding, concluded, "Will do."

It was as if a subtle frost had settled over their connection, and Paras, keenly aware, couldn't ignore the chill in the air. The unease that gripped him was compounded by the lack of clarity.   As Akshi's distance continued, Paras found it increasingly difficult to ignore the gnawing doubts in his mind. He began to wonder if he had ruined their beautiful friendship by revealing his feelings. Questions swirled in his mind like a tempest: What had triggered this change? Was it something he said, or was it an external factor shaping Akshi's actions?

Paras hooked with the uncertainty, his attempts to understand met with evasive maneuvers from Akshi. Each canceled plan, each unreturned call, felt like a small crack in the foundation of what they had built together. The dissonance between his lingering emotions and the growing distance left Paras in a state of emotional limbo.

(Several weeks later)

Paras, reaching out, initiated, "Hey, it's been a while since we've seen each other. Want to go out to lunch this weekend?"

Akshi, her tone a bit reserved, responded, "I'm not sure, Paras. Things have been a little weird between us recently."

Paras, a subtle knot forming in his stomach, inquired, "What exactly do you mean?"

Akshi, hesitating, admitted, "I've been feeling uneasy around you ever since you professed your feelings. I don't want to lose you as a friend, but I also don't want to lead you on."

Paras, a mix of disappointment and concern crossing his face, expressed, "I see your point of view, but I don't want things to get strange between us. Can't we just hang out like old times?"

Akshi, with a hint of vulnerability, responded, "I suppose we could give it a shot. But can we keep things simple for the time being?"

Paras, eager to find a middle ground, assured, "Yes, absolutely. I simply want to spend time with you, whether as friends or as more."

Akshi, softening, agreed, "Okay, that sounds excellent to me, but we'll meet later as I need some time."

Paras, understanding, said, "Sure, take your time."

In the midst of this chaotic period, Paras found himself thrust into a revelation that tore through him like a tempest, leaving in its wake shockwaves of jealousy and a disorienting fog of confusion. The revelation, that Akshi had been engrossed in conversations with another guy, unleashed an unexpected storm of emotions within Paras. Jealousy, like a relentless shadow, clung to him, becoming an unwelcome companion that intensified the turbulence within. Amidst this emotional tempest, a seemingly innocent exchange between Akshi and the mysterious guy became the catalyst for a blaze of insecurity within Paras. Each word exchanged and every laugh shared between them fueled the fire, turning a harmless connection into a source of torment for Paras. Fears and doubts, dormant but ever-present, rose to the surface, propelling Paras into a confrontation with Akshi that had long been brewing beneath the surface. The heated exchange that followed was a clash of emotions, a maelstrom of raw feelings that spilled out, unrestrained and unfiltered. Paras, driven by the whirlwind of his own insecurities, confronted Akshi with accusations that cut to the core of their connection. The air crackled with tension as regrettable words hung suspended, leaving an aftermath that echoed with the resonance of a shattered intimacy.

Paras, his tone tinged with frustration, expressed, "The fact that you'd do something like that is beyond me."

Akshi, defensively, retorted, "I'm not sure what you're on about, Paras."

Paras, cutting through the ambiguity, stated, "Spare me the act. I saw your text with that guy. You've been hanging out with him."

Akshi, growing frustrated, countered, "That's not accurate, Paras. He's just a friend, and we usually talk. And why did you check my phone?"

Paras, admitting his actions, explained, "I don't believe you. You were grinning and laughing like a little girl, and yeah, I checked your phone. It was an accident because your phone was open, and that guy's text popped up."

Akshi, trying to clarify, responded, "I can't control how I laugh, Paras. And why are you so envious in the first place? We're simply friends."

Paras, his voice tinged with hurt and frustration, questioned, "Friends? Is that all we are to you? I thought we had something special, Akshi. But if you're going to go around flirting with other guys, then maybe we should just stop talking altogether."

Akshi, her tone pleading, responded, "Paras, please don't say that. I didn't do anything wrong."

Paras, his emotions swirling, declared, "I don't want to hear it, Akshi. I need some time to think about things. Goodbye."

Akshi, a mix of desperation and concern, implored, "Paras, don't be silly."

After their big fight, Paras and Akshi decided to take a break from talking to each other for a month. This break left both of them feeling really messed up emotionally. The days felt super long, and the quietness between them created this heavy, empty feeling.

For Paras, this time-out was a chance to think about things. He had to figure out why he felt so jealous and scared of losing what he had with Akshi.

On the other side, Akshi was also dealing with her own confusing feelings, trying to understand why things got so tense between them all of a sudden. The month without talking turned out to be a real test for their relationship. It made them face the deeper problems that caused the fight in the first place. It was like they were standing on shaky ground, and they had to really think about how to make things right again.

This quiet month became a time for both Paras and Akshi to look inside themselves and see what was going on. They realized that their friendship was like a delicate balance, something that needed careful handling to keep it strong and healthy. As the days unfolded after the fight, Paras found himself in a kind of emptiness he couldn't ignore. It was like a missing piece in his life. The late-night calls with Akshi, the silence where their inside jokes used to be, and the lack of her texts throughout the day made him feel lost. The happiness and excitement Akshi brought into his life seemed to have disappeared, leaving behind a heavy emptiness and a sense of loss.

Paras struggled with a really tough feeling—that he might have messed up something really important. The memory of his jealousy and insecurities in their friendship hung over him, making him feel like he'd done something he couldn't undo. The thought of losing Akshi, who had become a big part of his life, was too painful to even think about. Nights became a cycle of restless replay, where he went over the fight again and again, looking for clues and answers that seemed to slip away. Trying to distract himself, Paras threw himself into his studies and hung out more with his friends.

Myra, who paid close attention, could see something was off. She noticed the distance that had crept into Paras's usual self, recognizing that something had changed in him.

One evening, Myra, her eyes filled with concern, gently approached Paras, "Paras, I've noticed that you haven't been yourself lately. Is everything okay?"

Paras let out a sigh, the weight of his emotions evident in his expression, "I had a fight with Akshi, Myra. It's been 3 months, and we haven't spoken since."

Myra's eyebrows furrowed with empathy, "What was the fight about?"

Paras hesitated, the memory of the conflict still vivid, "I got jealous when I saw her texting another guy. I accused her of flirting, and she denied it. But we ended up arguing, and I said some hurtful things. I don't know if I've ruined our friendship."

Myra placed a comforting hand on his shoulder, her voice soothing, "Paras, jealousy can be a tricky thing, but it's essential to communicate openly and honestly with Akshi. Tell her how you feel and apologize for any hurtful words you said. If your friendship is strong, you'll work through it."

"But what if I've already lost her?" Paras whispered; his voice tinged with sadness.

"You won't know until you try," Myra replied gently. "Reach out to her, be sincere, and give her the space she needs if she's still upset. A true friendship can withstand challenges like this." Myra's words carried a sense of hope, a reminder that sometimes, a heartfelt conversation could mend even the most broken connections.

Encouraged by Myra's advice, Paras took a deep breath and decided to follow through. Summoning his courage, he crafted a heartfelt message to Akshi, laying bare his feelings and expressing sincere regret for his actions. In his message, he emphasized the value he placed on their friendship and the emptiness he felt during their time apart. Paras admitted how much he missed her presence and the joy she brought into his life.

"Hey Akshi,

I hope you're doing okay. These months have given me a lot to ponder, and I really want to discuss what happened between us. I messed up, and I'm truly sorry for the hurtful things I said. My jealousy got the best of me, and I regret how it affected our friendship.

I miss our late-night calls, our inside jokes, and just having you around. You mean a lot to me, and I now realize how much I value our friendship. I don't want to lose that. I hope we can talk about this and find a way to move forward. I understand if you need time, but I just wanted you to know how much I miss you.

Take care,

Paras"

As he hit the send button, the minutes seemed to stretch into an agonizing eternity. Doubts and worries crept into Paras's mind, and the anticipation of Akshi's response weighed heavily on him. The fear that she might never reply loomed large, and he grappled with the uncertainty of whether their friendship could weather the storm he had unintentionally created.

Then, just when the wait felt almost unbearable, a message notification illuminated Paras's phone screen. The rush of relief and anticipation surged through him as he opened the message from Akshi. The words on the screen held the promise of a conversation, a lifeline that could potentially mend the fractures in their friendship.

"Hey Paras,

I appreciate your message, and I've also had some time to reflect on things. I appreciate your honesty and apology and miss our conversations too. I value our friendship as well, and I'm sorry too. Let's meet and talk."

After exchanging messages, Paras and Akshi decided to meet at their favorite café. As the time drew near, Paras felt a mix of relief and nerves. He wasn't sure what would happen, but he wanted to be honest with Akshi.

When they finally met, there was a bit of an awkward silence at first. But then, Akshi spoke up, "I never wanted to hurt you, Paras. You mean a lot to me, and I cherish our friendship. But I also need you to trust me and understand that I can have other friends too."

Paras nodded, "I know, Akshi. I'm sorry for jumping to conclusions and overreacting. It was my insecurity talking, and I shouldn't have taken it out on you."

Akshi sighed, "I was hurt by the things you said, but I also know that we're both human, and we make mistakes. I just want us to communicate better and not let misunderstandings come between us."

"I agree," Paras replied earnestly. "I never want to lose you as a friend, Akshi. You bring so much joy and laughter into my life, and I don't want to mess that up."

A small smile tugged at the corner of Akshi's lips, "I don't want to lose you either, Paras. We've been through so much together, and I value our friendship too much to let it go."

In that moment, Paras felt a weight lift off his chest. They had worked through their issues and reaffirmed their friendship. He knew that it would take time to rebuild the trust fully, but he was willing to put in the effort.

Paras was glad that they were able to sort things out, but he couldn't help but be upset when Akshi informed him that she had decided on a college that was far from his own. Akshi had made her choice assuming that Paras would never talk to her again. She was surprised to find that he had made the effort to call her and apologize.

Paras, with a hopeful tone, expressed, "I know you've made your college decision, but have you considered coming to the same one as me?"

Akshi, her voice carrying a mix of regret and explanation, responded, "I did think about it, but I already made a deposit at the other college. I thought you were never going to talk to me again, and I couldn't face you in the same college. Plus, I don't want our friendship to get in the way of our academics."

Paras, a tinge of sadness in his voice, said, "I understand, but it still makes me sad that we won't be able to spend as much time together."

Akshi, empathetic, replied, "I know, and I feel the same way. But we'll still see each other, right? We can plan weekends and breaks to hang out."

Paras, reassured but still wistful, said, "Of course. I just don't want to lose you as a friend, Akshi. You mean a lot to me."

Akshi, with sincerity, assured, "You won't lose me, Paras. I value our friendship too much to let distance get in the way. And who knows, maybe we'll end up in the same city with placements."

Paras, a genuine smile in his voice, responded, "Yeah, that would be amazing. Thanks for being there for me, Akshi. You're the best."

Akshi, laughing lightly, concluded, "You're pretty great too, Paras. And don't worry, I'll always be here for you." He felt a mix of emotions. Akshi had decided on a college that was far from his own, and while he was sad that they wouldn't be physically close, he knew that distance couldn't diminish the bond they had built. They promised to keep in touch, to visit each other whenever they could, and to continue supporting each other's dreams. Paras found solace in the fact that he had not lost Akshi completely and that their friendship remained intact, stronger than ever. With college looming on the horizon and the inevitability of parting ways, Paras and Akshi made a pact to savor every moment they had left together. Paras, aware that the clock was ticking down to the moment he would have to bid farewell to Akshi, grappled with the bittersweet reality. Despite having come to terms with the fact that their relationship wouldn't be taking a romantic turn, the prospect of Akshi leaving didn't make the impending goodbye any easier.

As they strolled together, Paras got engulfed in a cascade of memories, each step echoing with the laughter and conversations they had shared. The realization that their paths were about to diverge weighed heavily on him. He couldn't help but reflect on the countless times they had spent together, the deep talks that had woven the fabric of their connection, and the shared laughter that had painted their days with joy.

The impending farewell cast a shadow over Paras's thoughts. Although he had accepted the nature of their relationship, the prospect of a life without Akshi felt like an uncharted territory, and the gravity of her absence began to sink in. The quiet moments shared in their walks became a poignant backdrop to the looming goodbye, a collage of memories etched in Paras's mind, each one a testament to the depth of their connection. As he walked back home, lost in his thoughts, reflecting on the beautiful moments they had shared together.

"You really care about her, don't you?" he said to himself, as if trying to understand the depth of his emotions.

He knew that their friendship was something special, and he cherished the memories they had created. He couldn't deny the warmth and affection he still felt for Akshi, but he also understood that sometimes life had different plans for people.

"It might not be the romantic love I initially hoped for," he mused, "but it's a love nonetheless. A deep and genuine connection with someone who makes my days brighter." Paras understood the ebb and flow of life, recognizing that sometimes relationships take unexpected turns. Paras knew that their paths might diverge for a while, with Akshi going to a college far from his own. Still, he was determined to nurture their friendship and maintain their bond. As the days went by, their conversations continued, and he found solace in knowing that Akshi was just a call or text away.

"We promised to stay in touch," he reminded himself, "and I intend to keep that promise. Distance might separate us physically, but it won't weaken what we have."

"Love can take many forms," he thought, "and this friendship we have is no less meaningful. It's a love built on trust, laughter, and genuine care for each other."

He knew that the future was uncertain, but he was content knowing that Akshi would always hold a special place in his heart.

"No matter where life takes us," he said, looking up at the stars, "we'll always have this bond, and that's enough for me."

<u>Fighting for love</u>

"True love is not just about finding someone who loves you for who you are, but also someone who is willing to fight for you no matter what."

In the vast expanse of college life, where new faces and experiences collided, Paras found himself navigating the unfamiliar terrain with a constant companion in his thoughts, Akshi. Her absence cast a shadow over his days, and the echoes of their laughter seemed like distant whispers in the bustling corridors of his college. However, amidst the whirlwind of lectures, newfound friendships, and the vibrant chaos of campus life, Paras found solace in the nightly conversations that bridged the geographical gap between them. As the semesters unfolded, Paras noticed a subtle yet poignant shift in Akshi's digital presence. Her once-open window into daily adventures captured through the lens of Instagram stories suddenly seemed obscured. The warmth he once found in the glimpses of her life now became a source of puzzlement. Unable to view her updates, Paras felt an unexpected void. It wasn't just about missing the visual snippets of her days; it was the unspoken connection that those moments represented.

Amid this quiet confusion, an unease crept into his consciousness. His thoughts became a tempest, swirling with questions. Had something changed? Was there an unspoken shift between them? The distance, both physical and digital, became a chasm of uncertainty. Thoughts swirled in his mind, wondering if something had gone amiss between them. The curiosity gnawed at him until it got the better of him. Seeking guidance and a trusted close friend, Paras decided to share his concerns with Myra. He felt a vulnerable as he opened up to her, uncertain about what might be happening and whether it would impact the friendship they had cultivated over the years.

"Hey Myra," Paras began tentatively, "I've noticed something strange with Akshi's social media. I can't view her Instagram stories anymore, and it's making me a bit uneasy. Do you think something might be wrong between us?" Paras confided in Myra, hoping for some insight or reassurance that could put his restless thoughts to rest.

Myra looked at him with a knowing expression. "Oh, so you finally noticed, huh?"

Paras raised an eyebrow, confused. "Noticed what?"

Myra chuckled. "Akshi blocked you from seeing her Instagram stories, but she didn't block me. I guess she didn't want you to know about her dating someone else."

The words hit Paras like a sudden storm, stirring up a whirlwind of emotions - hurt, jealousy, and a palpable sense of loss. The realization that Akshi might be romantically involved with someone else caught him off guard. Despite the rational part of him acknowledging that he had no right to feel this way, an undeniable pang of unease settled in his chest. The concept of Akshi dating someone else felt like a silent echo of being replaced, a notion he hadn't anticipated.

"I had no idea she was seeing someone," Paras muttered, grappling with the weight of the revelation as he tried to process the sudden shift in their dynamic.

Myra, sensing his turmoil, placed a comforting hand on his shoulder. "Look, I know it's tough, but maybe you should talk to her about it. Communication is key, and you need to be honest with her about how you feel."

Paras nodded, appreciating Myra's support. Later that day, armed with a mix of apprehension and determination, he mustered the courage to call Akshi and address the newfound information. "Hey, Akshi, can we talk?" Paras asked, striving to maintain steadiness in his voice.

"Sure, what's up?" Akshi replied, sounding casual, unaware of the storm brewing on the other end of the line.

Paras took a deep breath, the weight of his words heavy in the air. "Myra told me that you're dating someone. Is that true?" There was a momentary silence on the other end of the line, a pregnant pause that hung in the air before Akshi responded. "Yes, it's true. I didn't want to bring it up because I didn't want things to get awkward between us." The admission carried a hint of hesitation, a recognition of the potential impact this revelation might have on their friendship.

"I understand," he responded, his voice carrying a tone of acceptance. "I just want you to be happy." The simplicity of his words masked the complexity of his feelings. Paras, despite the twinge of disappointment, recognized the importance of Akshi's happiness and the need for their friendship to evolve with the changing dynamics. In uttering those words, Paras conveyed a depth of maturity and selflessness. His desire for Akshi's happiness took precedence over any personal sentiments, illustrating a genuine concern for her well-being. It was a testament to the resilience of their friendship, even in the face of unexpected turns. After his conversation with Akshi, Paras felt a mix of emotions swirling inside him. He shared the details with Myra, feeling a bit defeated by the current situation. He couldn't shake off the sadness that enveloped him, and memories of a similar incident from the past resurfaced in his mind. Myra listened attentively, understanding the turmoil Paras was going through. She knew how much he cared for Akshi and how deeply their friendship meant to him.

"You remember when we had a similar situation back in college, right?" Myra said gently, referring to a time when Paras had faced a similar heartache with a different girl.

Paras nodded, his gaze drifting into the distance. "Yeah, I do. I guess I can't help but feel like history is repeating itself."

Myra comforting him. "Paras, I know it's tough, but you have to remember that things are not always in our control. People's feelings and circumstances can change, and sometimes we can't do anything about it. All we can do is cherish the memories and the beautiful moments we shared."

"I know," Paras sighed, "but it hurts, Myra. I thought our bond was strong enough to withstand anything."

"It still is," Myra reassured him. "Akshi is going through her own journey, and maybe she needs some space to figure things out. But that doesn't mean she doesn't value your friendship."

"I want to believe that," Paras said softly, "but it's hard not to feel replaced, you know?"

Myra gave him a sympathetic look. "I understand, but you can't compare yourself to anyone else. Your friendship with Akshi is unique, and it's built on genuine care and trust. Don't let insecurity cloud what you two have."

Paras nodded, taking in Myra's words. "You're right. I just need to give her space and time, and if we're meant to be together, we'll find our way back to each other."

"That's the spirit," Myra said with a warm smile. "And in the meantime, remember that I'm here for you, no matter what."

As the days passed, Paras navigated the delicate balance of giving Akshi the space she needed while maintaining his role as a supportive friend. Immersing himself in his studies and hobbies became a therapeutic outlet, a way to channel his energy and focus on personal growth. Myra, a constant presence in his life, continued to offer unwavering support, serving as his close friend and pillar of strength. Then, out of the blue, Akshi's call disrupted the rhythm of Paras's routine. The initial pleasantries masked an underlying tension, setting the stage for a revelation that would shift the dynamics of their friendship.

Akshi, with a thoughtful tone, initiated, "Hey Paras, how are you doing?"

Paras, genuine in his response, shared, "I'm doing okay, thanks for asking. How about you?"

Akshi, a hint of anticipation in her voice, continued, "I'm good too. Listen, there's something I wanted to talk to you about."
Paras, his confusion palpable, asked, "What is it?"

Akshi had recently broken up. As she shared the details of her breakup, Paras listened with surprise.

Akshi, choosing her words carefully, began, "So, I know that I told you I was dating someone in college, but things didn't work out between us."

Paras, his curiosity piqued, responded, "I see."

Akshi, with a mix of uncertainty and sincerity, continued, "Yeah, and I've been thinking a lot about us lately. I realized that I still have feelings for you."

On one hand, there was a flicker of happiness that Akshi was single again, but on the other hand, Paras grappled with a complicated set of emotions trying to process the situation. The weight of the situation hung in the air as Paras grappled with conflicting emotions. While part of him felt a sense of validation, another part couldn't shake the shadow of being perceived as a second choice someone she turned to when things didn't work out with someone else. The intricacies of their friendship had taken an unexpected turn, leaving Paras in a contemplative state, unsure of how to navigate the evolving dynamics.

As Akshi laid bare her feelings, Paras found himself caught in a moment of contemplation. The weight of her words hung in the air, and a pause lingered as he carefully chose his response.

Paras, his thoughts swirling, expressed, "I appreciate your honesty, Akshi. It's just... it's a lot to process."

A contemplative pause followed before Paras continued, "Akshi, I don't know if I'm ready to dive back into anything more than friendship with you just yet."
Akshi, with a touch of disappointment, responded, "I understand that, Paras. But I really want to make things work between us. I think we have something special."

Paras acknowledged the uniqueness of their connection, but the complexities of their history couldn't be easily brushed aside.

Paras, somberly acknowledging the changes of their situation, shared, "I know we do, Akshi. But it's just hard for me to forget about everything that's happened between us. I need some time to process everything."

Akshi, realizing the weight of his words, responded with a mix of hope and concern, "I get it. I just hope that you'll give us a chance eventually."

Paras, his voice softened with the need for personal growth and introspection, conveyed, "(softly) Akshi, I need time to do what's best for me right now."

Akshi, recognizing the gravity of his words, sighed but remained supportive, saying, "Okay, I understand. Just know that I'll be here for you, no matter what."

Paras, offering a faint smile that carried gratitude for her understanding, replied, "(smiles slightly) Thanks, Akshi. I appreciate that." In this exchange, he delicately navigated the complexities of their evolving relationship. While Akshi hoped for a rekindling of their connection, Paras prioritized his own emotional well-being and the necessity of time to process the intricate layers of their shared history. The future remained uncertain, but both acknowledged the importance of understanding and respect in preserving the essence of their bond.

As the days went by, Paras tried his best to navigate his emotions and maintain a friendly relationship with Akshi. He appreciated her honesty about her feelings, but he needed time to figure out what he wanted and what was best for him. However, as he tried to keep his distance, Akshi's behavior towards him started to change. She seemed frustrated and annoyed, and her words became harsher. One day, she called him up and confronted him in a way he didn't expect.

Akshi, with a serious tone, initiated, "Paras, we need to talk."

Paras, nervously, responded, "Sure, what's on your mind?"

Akshi, frustration evident in her voice, expressed, "I don't understand why you're making such a big deal out of this. We could have something great together, but you keep holding back."

Paras, seeking honesty and transparency, attempted to convey his need for time, saying, "Akshi, it's not that simple. I need time to figure things out; a lot has happened, and I don't want to rush into anything."

Akshi, angry, retorted, "Well, it feels like you're just leading me on. If you're not interested, then just say it."

Paras, defensive, asserted, "I'm not leading you on. I'm just being honest about how I feel."

Akshi, sarcastic, responded, "Oh, how noble of you. Spare me the drama, Paras. If you're thinking you're so special in my life, you're not anymore."

Paras, hurt, pleaded, "Akshi! I never said that. I care about you, and all I'm asking is for you to give us time. I need time, Akshi."

Akshi, angry, declared, "You know what? Let's just end this. I thought you were serious about me, and now you're dodging my feelings. Don't talk to me ever again, Paras."

As Akshi's harsh words echoed through the phone, Paras felt an unexpected pang of pain in his heart. The intensity of her reaction caught him off guard, and the hurtful comments left an emotional wound that ran deep. The weight of her words settled like a heavy stone in the pit of his stomach, intensifying the emotional turmoil he was already grappling with. Paras had approached the situation with a genuine desire for honesty and transparency, never anticipating that it would lead to such a bad response. The unexpected turn of events left him feeling vulnerable and exposed, as if the ground beneath him had shifted unpredictably.

The pang of pain reverberated through Paras, leaving him in a state of emotional distress. He hadn't expected Akshi, someone he had shared a deep connection with, to react with anger and sarcasm. The hurtful nature of her comments intensified emotions he was experiencing, plunging him into a deeper sense of sadness and introspection. The unexpected turn of events had taken a toll on his emotional well-being, leaving him to grapple with the aftermath of a fractured friendship and the harsh reality of unanticipated consequences. In the following days, they stopped talking to each other, and Paras found himself feeling lonelier than ever. He missed their conversations, their laughter, and the connection they had. But he also knew that he couldn't be with Akshi just because he felt guilty or pressured into it.

He confided in Myra about everything, and she reminded him that he had to prioritize his own feelings and well-being. It was a difficult time for Paras, but he knew he had to stay strong and true to himself. As the weeks passed, Paras focused on healing and finding his own happiness. He immersed himself in his studies, spent time with friends, and pursued his hobbies. Slowly, the pain started to fade, and he realized that he deserved someone who would understand and respect his feelings, just as he would do for them and as time went on, Paras began to accept that he and Akshi were on different paths. He cherished the memories they had shared but knew that it was time to let go and move forward.

Life had taught him that not every bond was meant to last forever, and sometimes, the most important relationship to nurture was the one he had with himself. And with that newfound realization, Paras embraced his own journey, hopeful for the love and happiness that awaited him in the future.

Months went by, and Paras slowly started to move on, focusing on himself. But he always feels like he had lost something special with Akshi. He didn't know if they would ever be able to go back.

<u>Trying to move on</u>

"When one door of happiness closes, another opens; but often we look so long at the closed door that we do not see the one which has been opened for us."

- Helen Keller

Sometimes in life we become so focused on what we have lost or what is no longer available to us that we fail to recognize new opportunities and possibilities that arise. It is human nature to feel attached to things or people that we have lost, but this can also prevent us from moving on and finding new sources of happiness.

As the days melted into weeks and stretched into months, Paras found himself engulfed in an overwhelming sadness, a heavy cloak that clung to him persistently. The aftermath of a significant fight with Akshi had left him feeling as if a fragment of himself had crumbled away. The absence she chose felt like a void, and its weight pressed down on Paras, making him profoundly disheartened.

Engulfed in this emotional storm, the things that once brought joy lost their glow. The invitations from friends and attempts by Myra to lift his spirits seemed weak against the gravity of his sadness. Even the comforting gestures failed to pierce through the dense fog of sadness that had settled around him. One evening, as the shadows deepened and silence enveloped his room, Paras sat alone, his thoughts a turbulent sea of reflections on the cascade of events. It was in this tearful solitude that a gentle knock echoed, and his sister Sachi, adjusted to the sadness that had wrapped around her brother, entered the room.

Sachi noticed that Paras looked really sad, like a dark cloud was hanging over him. She sat down next to him and asked, "Hey, what's been going on with you lately? You seem different, and I can tell something is bothering you."

Paras didn't know if he should talk about it, but then he thought maybe sharing would help. "It's nothing, Sachi. I'm just going through a rough patch."

Sachi didn't buy it; she knew her brother well. "Come on, Paras. We've always been there for each other. You can talk to me. Is it about Akshi?"

Paras looked down, feeling a bit relieved that he didn't have to keep it all inside. "Yeah, it's about Akshi. We had a falling out, and it's been tough for me to cope with it."

Sachi understood and put a hand on his shoulder. "I'm sorry to hear that, Paras. Losing someone you love even when there is no romantic thing involved, can be incredibly painful. But you know, sometimes things don't work out, and it's okay. You can't force someone to stay in your life."

Paras nodded, feeling a tear rolling down his cheek. "I know, but I can't help feeling like it's my fault. Yeah, it's my fault that I would have said yes to her but I really needed time because she dated a guy and then she came back. I really wanted to give us time after that or Maybe I shouldn't have said anything about my feelings for her earlier."

Sachi shook her head gently. "Paras, you can't blame yourself for being honest about your feelings. It takes a lot of courage to open up like that. But remember, you can't control how someone else feels or what they choose to do. What matters now is how you handle the aftermath.

Paras sniffled, wiping away his tears. "I just miss her so much and now she's gone."

Sachi hugged him, offering comfort. "I understand, and it's okay to grieve the loss of that person. But don't forget that you have people who care about you, including me. I'll always be here for you, no matter what. And remember, you're not alone in this. Lean on your friends and family for support."

In the following weeks, he slowly started opening up to his friends and family about his feelings, and he sought professional help to deal with his depression. It was a challenging journey, but he began to see glimpses of hope and healing. Myra continued to be his rock, providing a listening ear and unwavering support. Paras slowly started to piece himself back together after the tough times with Akshi. He decided to focus on making himself happier and better. Paras got into personal development, trying out new things he never thought he would, and rediscovering the things that made him feel alive. It wasn't an instant change, but bit by bit, he began to feel the weight of sadness lifting, and a genuine smile returning to his face.

Through the pain and heartbreak, Paras found a strength inside him that he never knew existed. Even though the scars of the past were still there, he was determined to face life with an open heart and a new appreciation for letting go of things that weighed him down. As he moved ahead, Paras carried the lessons of self-love and resilience with him. He knew that healing wasn't something that happened overnight, but he was ready to take on the journey with courage and grace, understanding that he became stronger and wiser because of it. But, no matter how hard he tried, thoughts of Akshi lingered in his mind. Every attempt to push her out seemed to bring her back, making him wonder what might have happened if he never shared his feelings. For months, Paras tried everything to move on. He went on a few dates, focused on his work, and even hit the gym regularly. Yet, the thoughts of Akshi persisted, proving that moving on was easier said than done.

No matter how much Paras tried to move on, the feeling of losing someone special lingered like a stubborn shadow. As he got ready for the gym, he made a conscious effort to push thoughts of Akshi out of his mind. The realization that he needed to move forward echoed in his thoughts, but the process was proving to be much more challenging than he expected. Every step he took, every girl he met, seemed to draw parallels to Akshi, creating an involuntary comparison that played on a loop in his mind.

"I know I shouldn't keep dwelling on Akshi, but it's like she's stuck in my mind. I can't seem to shake her off, no matter how hard I try. Maybe going to the gym will help me clear my head."

At the gym, Paras threw himself into his workout with determination. He lifted weights, ran on the treadmill, and pushed his body to the limit. The physical exertion offered a temporary reprieve, providing a brief escape from the persistent thoughts of Akshi. In those moments, surrounded by the clatter of weights and the rhythmic thud of his own footsteps, Paras found a fleeting sense of clarity. However, as soon as he left the gym and headed back home, the floodgates of memories opened, and thoughts of Akshi rushed back in. Determined to redirect his focus, Paras immersed himself in his work, a significant project demanding his attention. Yet, every attempt to concentrate proved futile, as his mind persistently wandered back to Akshi. The weight of her absence seemed to infiltrate every corner of his thoughts, making it challenging to escape the gravitational pull of their shared past.

Leaving the gym one day, Paras unexpectedly ran into a girl from his past, someone he had known from school but hadn't seen in years. As they engaged in conversation, he felt a connection, and despite his reservations about diving back into the dating scene, he agreed to go for a drink with her. The evening turned out to be enjoyable, and Paras liked her company. However, the moment he returned home, thoughts of Akshi resurfaced.

"Why do I keep comparing every girl I meet to Akshi? It's not fair to them or to me. I need to focus on getting to know them for who they are, not for who they're not."

The cycle seemed unbreakable. He met new people, attempted to move forward, but inevitably drawing comparisons to Akshi. He recognized the need to break free from this pattern but struggled to discern how. Over time, he began to realize that he was holding onto something that had reached its natural conclusion. Akshi had moved on, and he needed to do the same. Waiting for her return was only holding him back.

"I hate feeling like I'm stuck in limbo, waiting for something that might never happen. But at the same time, I can't imagine moving on from Akshi. It's like I'm caught between a rock and a hard place."

To channel his energy positively, he intensified his gym routine, pushing himself to new limits. The focus shifted from waiting to becoming the best version of himself. Gradually, he started feeling better. Although he resumed going on dates, this time, the experience was different. He wasn't measuring these new connections against the ghost of

Akshi; he was appreciating them for their unique qualities without dwelling on what might have been.

"Every time I see a happy couple, it reminds me of what I don't have with Akshi. It's like a constant reminder of what I lost. But maybe it's time to start focusing on my own happiness, instead of what I don't have."

"I wish I could just turn off my feelings for Akshi like a switch. But it's not that easy. I care about her so much, and it hurts to know that she's moved on while I'm still stuck in the same place."

As he continued his routine at the gym, the familiar hum of exercise equipment surrounding him, he heard a voice that sent a jolt of surprise through his entire being. Turning around, there she was Akshi. The disbelief etched on his face mirrored the mix of emotions swirling within him. Months had passed since their last encounter, and running into her at the gym was a twist of fate he never anticipated.

Akshi, catching Paras's gaze, greeted him with a small smile, "Hey, fancy meeting you here." Her voice carried both surprise and warmth.

Paras, still processing the unexpected reunion, managed to stammer out a response, "Uh, yeah. Hi, Akshi. Long time no see.

A soft chuckle escaped Akshi's lips, "Yeah, it's been a while. How have you been?"

Paras hesitated, unsure of how much to reveal. "I've had my ups and downs, but I'm doing okay now."

Understanding flickered in Akshi's eyes as she nodded, "I'm sorry things got so complicated between us."

"It's okay," Paras replied, attempting to maintain composure. "Life can be unpredictable sometimes."

An awkward yet nostalgic silence lingered between them. Akshi seemed to be searching for the right words, but before she could speak, Myra walked into the gym and spotted them.

"Hey, look who we have here!" Myra exclaimed with a grin. "Long time no see, Akshi!"

Returning Myra's smile, Akshi's expression carried a subtle unease, "Hi, Myra. It's good to see you too."

Myra, sensing the tension between Paras and Akshi, proposed a solution, "Well, this is a pleasant surprise. How about we all grab a coffee after the workout? We can catch up."

Paras hesitated for a moment, uncertain if he was ready for that. Before he could decline, Akshi spoke up, "Sure, that sounds nice. I'd love to catch up." As they sat at the coffee shop, the initial awkwardness slowly gave way to a more relaxed atmosphere. Myra did most of the talking, sharing funny stories and updates about her life. Paras noticed that Akshi seemed a bit reserved, but he appreciated her effort to be there.

As they prepared to leave, Akshi turned to Paras. "I'm sorry for everything, Paras. I never meant to hurt you. The thing is, I was really hurt by that guy, and I wanted someone to comfort me, but that frustration took a different turn."

Paras took a deep breath, finding his voice. "I appreciate that, Akshi. It's been tough, but I understand that things happen."

She looked at him with sincerity in her eyes. "You were always such a good friend to me."

Paras smiled softly. "Friends make mistakes too, Akshi. I'm not perfect either. But I'm sorry too for everything that happened between us. I know I hurt you, and I regret that. But I want you to know that I value our friendship, and I don't want to lose you."

Akshi returned a soft smile. "I appreciate that, Paras. But I think we both need to move on and focus on our own lives for a while. We can still be friends, but maybe it's time for us to take a step back from each other for a bit."

Paras nodded, feeling a lump form in his throat. "Yeah, maybe you're right. It's just hard, you know? I keep thinking about you all the time.

"I know," Akshi said, placing a hand on his shoulder. "But you can't keep living in the past. You need to focus on your own happiness, too."

As they talked, Paras realized that he no longer felt the same way he had before. He was genuinely happy for her, seeing that she was doing well. Paras nodded, a sense of determination washing over him. Perhaps it was time for him to start moving on. However, as he walked away from Akshi, a part of him still clung to the hope that they would someday be together again. Paras felt like he was back at square one, having tried to move on, yet the lingering emotions persisted.

Akshi again had brought back all the old feelings.

He watched as Akshi walked away, her figure gradually becoming smaller in the distance. It was a simple encounter, a few exchanged words, yet it had stirred up a whirlwind of emotions within him. The hug was comforting, her words reassuring, but underneath it all was a bittersweet feeling that he couldn't shake.

The sound of Akshi's voice lingered in Paras's mind, echoing her genuine inquiry about his well-being. How could he articulate the intricate web of thoughts and emotions stirring within him? As Akshi turned the corner and disappeared from sight, Paras found himself replaying their shared history. The laughter, the late-night conversations, the shared dreams—each memory vivid in his mind. He had naively believed that time and distance could aid in moving on, consigning these feelings to the past. Yet, Akshi's sudden reappearance shattered that illusion.

Seeing her again brought forth a flood of emotions, emotions he thought were under control. It wasn't merely about missing her presence; it was about yearning for what could have been. The haunting questions of what-ifs and maybes tormented him—what if he had acted differently, what if their timing had aligned?

The hug, a simple embrace between friends, felt like a lifeline, a connection to their shared past. A past overshadowed by confusion and misunderstandings but still lingering beneath the surface.

"Paras?"

His sister's voice cut through his thoughts. Sachi gazed at him, concern etched on her face. Familiar with his moods, she sensed when something was amiss.

"Are you alright?" she inquired, her eyes searching his.

Paras nodded, conjuring a smile. "Yeah, I'm fine. Just lost in thought."

Observing him, Sachi spoke gently, "You know, Paras, I've noticed a change in you lately. You've been distant, preoccupied. And I think I have an inkling of what might be causing it."

Sighing, Paras realized he couldn't conceal his feelings from her. "It's just... complicated, Sachi."

She placed a comforting hand on his shoulder. "I get it, Paras. Sometimes the heart doesn't follow a logical path. But you have to ask yourself what you really want."

The question lingered in his mind, haunting him with its uncertainty. What did he want? Since Akshi reentered his life, it had been echoing relentlessly. Did he want to strive to move on, preserving their friendship on that level? Or did he yearn to explore the potential for something more, despite the risks it entailed?

Gazing at the spot where Akshi had vanished, Paras grappled with the realization that answers wouldn't come easily. The path ahead seemed uncertain, and his heart was in turmoil. One thing was clear: suppressing his feelings was no longer an option. Whether it led to a renewed friendship or something more, confronting his emotions became a necessity. He needed to decipher what truly lay in his heart.

Realizing the urgency to untangle his emotions, he headed home. Attempting to distract himself with TV and video games, the feeling of sadness lingered. In the weeks that followed, Akshi occupied his thoughts more and more. The gym became a sanctuary, a place to escape and, perhaps, to forget. Paras acknowledged the need to shift focus to himself and his happiness.

Taking proactive steps, he delved into new hobbies. Joining a book club and exploring the realm of painting became his outlets. Despite these efforts to distract himself, Paras found himself trapped in the past. The ache of missing Akshi persisted, and he couldn't shake the constant wonder did she think about him too?

<u>Running into her</u>

"I never believed in fate until the day I ran into her."

-Paras

In an attempt to break free from the shadows of the past, Paras found solace in the world of literature. Joining a local book club became his refuge, introducing him to the diverse landscapes of storytelling. As he delved into the pages of novels and immersed himself in the beauty of words, Paras discovered a new form of self-expression poetry.

One evening, inspired by the poetic verses he encountered in the books he read, Paras decided to try his hand at crafting shayari and poems. He sat by his window, gazing at the moonlit sky, and let his emotions spill onto the pages. With each carefully chosen word, he unraveled the intricacies of his heart, transforming pain into verses that echoed with a poignant melody.

"I wish I was the only one she met before

I wish I was the only one she loved before

I wish I was the only one she's been waiting for

I wish she's reading this, thinking why I never met him before"

The act of writing became a cathartic release for Paras. Through the rhythmic flow of words, he found a channel to navigate his emotions and reflect on the journey he had undertaken. The book club meetings became a platform for him to share his creations, and surprisingly, the members resonated with the raw authenticity of his verses. He continued to explore the world of poetry; he not only found a creative outlet but also a community that appreciated the beauty of introspection through words. Through his newfound hobby, he began to redefine his identity and discovered a source of strength that went beyond the confines of his past. Poetry became not just an art form but a companion on his journey towards self-discovery and healing. The book club decided to organize an open mic event, allowing members to showcase their literary talents. Paras hesitated at first, unsure whether he was ready to unveil the vulnerable pieces of his soul to an audience. However, fueled by a newfound courage, he decided to share his shayari and poems. The night of the open mic arrived, and Paras took the stage with a mix of nervousness and anticipation. As he began reciting his verses, a hush fell over the room. The raw emotion woven into his words resonated with the audience, creating an intimate connection that transcended the boundaries of spoken language.

"Kuch waqt hi toh maanga tha tumse,

Tumse yun, tumhara hone ke liye,

Hum intezaar mein yun baithe the,

Tumhari raah takte huye,

Par waqt guzra, haazar gile-shikwe hue,

Shayad galti humari hi thi,

Warna jaana yun laazmi toh nahi tha,

Abhi bhi sochta hoon, kya galat tha mein ya bas waqt ki numaaish thi,

Par zaalim waqt ne humse khudko hi cheen liya,

Magar kuch waqt hi toh maanga tha tumse,

Sirf tumse, tumhara hone ke liye."

To his surprise, the applause that followed was thunderous, echoing the appreciation of those who had been touched by his sincerity. Members of the book club approached him afterward, expressing gratitude for the authenticity he brought to the literary community.

Among the audience was Myra, who had always been a supporter of Paras's journey to self-discovery.

She approached him with a warm smile and said, "Paras, I had no idea you had such a way with words. Your poetry captures the essence of human emotion in a way that's truly captivating."

Encouraged by the positive reception, Paras continued to explore different themes and styles in his writing. The act of penning down his feelings allowed him to confront the complexities of his emotions surrounding Akshi. The poetry became a medium through which he could articulate the beauty of love, loss, and the process of healing. As he shared his verses in subsequent book club meetings, he noticed a change within himself. The weight of the past began to lift, and the act of creating something beautiful from the fragments of heartache became a therapeutic journey.

A few days later, Paras found himself back at the familiar café, catching up with a friend over coffee. As he chatted about life and shared laughter, his eyes wandered to a nearby table, and there she was Akshi, sitting alone with a book in hand. His friend, sensing the unspoken turmoil within Paras, nudged him gently.

"Go on, man. You've got this," the friend encouraged, recognizing the unresolved emotions written across Paras's face.

Summoning a deep breath and pushing aside the waves of uncertainty, Paras decided to approach Akshi. With each step, he could feel the weight of their shared history and the unresolved questions lingering in the air.

"Hey, Akshi," he greeted, attempting a casual tone though his emotions were anything but. "It's been a while."

Akshi looked up, her guarded expression meeting his gaze. Time had woven subtle changes into her appearance, yet the essence of the feelings Paras held for her remained steadfast.

"Hi, paras," she responded, her tone reserved. "Just taking a break from college work." He settled into the seat across from her, a palpable mixture of awkwardness and uncertainty filled the air. This moment, long yearned for, held the weight of unspoken history, and Paras felt the echoes of their past reverberate in the silence.

"I've missed you," he admitted "and I was thinking if we can be in a long-distance relationship because I don't want to lose you!" the words slipping out before he could gauge their impact. Akshi's eyes widened slightly; a flicker of surprise evident on her face. She seemed caught off guard, struggling to find the right response.

"Paras, I believe it's better for both of us if we don't continue seeing each other," she asserted, her tone firm, gaze unwavering. "I've moved forward, and I think it's best for you to do the same and I don't want to be in a long-distance relationship because I don't like that." The weight of her words hit Paras like a sudden blow, the reality of her decision crashing down on him. He had hoped for a chance, a possibility that their connection could withstand the tests of time and change. Yet, Akshi was resolute in her determination to sever their bond. With an effort, Paras managed a nod, his voice carrying a note of acceptance.

"I understand. I just wanted you to know that my feelings for you haven't changed."

For a fleeting moment, Akshi's gaze held his, revealing a a mix of emotions.. It was as if she, too, was wrestling with the echoes of their shared history. But then, she averted her eyes and rose from her seat. "It's time for me to go," she stated, gathering her belongings. "Take care, Paras."

As she left the café, Paras sat there, grappling with a storm of feelings. The reunion he had envisioned had taken an unexpected turn, leaving him to navigate a sea of uncharted feelings and unanswered questions. The vulnerability he had exposed, the emotions he had laid bare, seemed to have only widened the chasm between them. It dawned on him that the path to healing and moving on would be a challenging one, and his heart would require time to mend from the ache of unrequited love. Remaining seated at the café, Paras found himself lost in his thoughts, contemplating the intricate complex web of feelings and relationships. It was a harsh realization that, despite his earnest efforts, he couldn't dictate Akshi's choices. However, he could control his response to the aftermath of their connection. With a steadying breath, he made a silent promise to himself to gather the shattered fragments of his heart and forge ahead, even if it meant closing a chapter of his life that had once held profound significance.

Whereas Akshi, In the quiet confines of her room, found herself surrounded by the remnants of their shared memories. Photographs, tokens of affection, and handwritten notes that had once brought joy now served as sad reminders of what they once were a duo entangled in the beautiful yet intricate dance of friendship and something more. The letter she had penned for Paras lay on the table, its words etched with both resolve and regret. The intention behind her actions had been rooted in the belief that a clean break was necessary for the healing process to commence. Yet, as she revisited the contents of the letter, a knot of uncertainty tightened in her stomach.

"Dear Paras,

I hope this letter finds you when things are a bit calmer, but I know the words I'm about to write might not bring peace. My heart feels heavy as I put these words down; it's like the weight goes beyond the ink on this paper. I want to thank you for the beautiful moments we've had, the laughter, the understanding, and the real connection we shared. Those memories are precious, and I'll hold onto them even as we head in different directions. The reason I'm writing this letter is to tell you about a decision that's been really hard for me. I've spent many nights thinking about what lies ahead, and the clarity I'm searching for often feels hard to grasp. Our connection, as wonderful as it is, has become complicated in ways we didn't expect.

I want you to know that my decision comes from a belief that a clean break is needed for both of us to heal. I don't want either of us stuck in the uncertainty of 'what if' and 'maybe,' which can sometimes be more painful than making a clear decision.

Yet, as I read over these words, I know they might hit hard.

My decision might seem harsh, and for that, I'm truly sorry. I never wanted to hurt you, and knowing I might have is a burden I carry. I hope you find the strength to deal with the mix of emotions that might come. While I wish you peace, I also know that decisions like these come with a lot of uncertainty. Time might help bring understanding that seems far away now.

Please know that my choice isn't meant to say you're not important. It's about recognizing that we both need to go on our own journeys of growing and figuring ourselves out.

I hope the paths we choose lead us both to the happiness we're searching for.

With sincere regards,

Akshi"

Although she never gave the letter to him for not leading him on despite the undeniable connection she shared with Paras, Akshi grappled with a sense of skepticism when it came to the prospect of a long-distance relationship. His presence had been a source of comfort, a completeness she cherished, yet the uncertainty inherent in maintaining their connection across miles cast a shadow of doubt.

"I care about Paras deeply, and his presence has always brought comfort and joy into my life. But these miles between us, they feel like an insurmountable obstacle. Can love withstand the complexities of long-distance relationships?"

Akshi's skepticism stemmed from a fear of leading Paras

down a path filled with challenges and potential heartbreak. The intricacies of a long-distance relationship loomed large in her mind, and she couldn't shake the concern that the hurdles they might face could eclipse the joy they once found in each other's company.

"I can't shake the fear that leading Paras into this uncertainty might hurt him more in the end. What if the challenges eclipse the happiness we once shared? I can't bear the thought of causing him pain. It's not about a lack of love. If anything, it's because I care so much that I'm taking this step. I want to shield him from potential heartbreak, protect him from the struggles that come with distance."

"Matters of the heart are fragile, and I need to be realistic. Maybe, in time, he'll understand that this decision was made out of love, a difficult choice to ensure his well-being. I just hope he sees the care behind the distance."

Paras on the other hand was completely shattered and called Myra, and told everything that happened

Paras's reliable close friend picked up the phone on the first ring, sensing the urgency in his voice. "Paras, what's wrong?" she asked, concern lacing her words.

Paras took a deep breath, his voice heavy with emotion. "Akshi... she ended it, Myra. She wants us to go our separate ways."

There was a brief silence on the other end as Myra processed the weight of his words. "I'm so sorry, Paras. I know how much she meant to you. What happened?"

Paras recounted the encounter at the café, the words exchanged, and the finality of Akshi's decision. Myra listened attentively, offering words of comfort and understanding.

"She said it's for the best, Myra. But it hurts so much. I thought we could make it work, even if it's long distance," Paras admitted, the pain evident in his voice.

Myra sighed, empathizing with her friend's turmoil. "Sometimes, people have their reasons, and it's tough to change their minds. But I'm here for you, Paras. We'll get through this together." After listening saying this, Myra let out a sigh. "Paras, I understand that you're hurting, but expressing your feelings to Akshi might have been a bit too much. You should have moved on from her by now."

Paras felt a twinge of guilt, knowing that Myra had a point. "I just couldn't hold it in, Myra. I needed her to know how I felt."

Myra, in her straightforward way, scolded him gently. "Look, I get it, but sometimes you need to prioritize your own well-being. If she's moved on, you should too. Dwelling on it like this won't help you heal."

Paras nodded, reluctantly. "I know you're right, Myra. It's just harder than I thought it would be."

Myra's tone softened. "I know, Paras. But you're strong, and I believe you'll get through this. Give yourself some time, maybe it's time for you to explore new connections. Go out, talk to other people, or even consider going on a date. Who knows, you might find someone genuine and create new, beautiful memories. And try to stop thinking about Akshi you'll find better than her."

Paras hesitated at the idea, still tethered to the memories of Akshi. "I don't know if I'm ready for that, Myra."

Myra encouraged him with a reassuring smile. "Moving on doesn't mean forgetting. It's about opening yourself up to new possibilities. You deserve happiness, Paras, and sometimes, it comes from unexpected places."

Paras pondered Myra's words, contemplating the idea of stepping out of his comfort zone. Perhaps it was time to let go of the past and embrace the potential for a brighter future.

The Rebound

"Rebounds are like jumping on a trampoline - it may give you a temporary high, but eventually, you'll come back down."

Paras basked in the liberation that came with releasing the weight of his past with Akshi. The burdens that once dragged him down were replaced with a newfound lightness, offering him a fresh outlook on life. The future unfolded before him like an unwritten story, filled with endless possibilities, and he eagerly embraced it. Entering his office building first day of his internship, Paras carried with him a revitalized spirit, a sense of energy, and optimism that seemed to radiate from within. Little did he know that life had its own plans, ready to weave unexpected threads into the fabric of his journey. As he navigated through the corridors of his professional life, Paras encountered a new presence Vartika, a vibrant and charismatic colleague. Her aura exuded an infectious energy that acted like a magnetic force, drawing Paras into her orbit. Each interaction with Vartika became a highlight of his day, and he found himself eagerly anticipating the moments they shared.

Paras smiled warmly as he approached Vartika, his heart

upbeat by her welcoming appearance. "Hey, Vartika! Mind if I join you at the coffee machine?"

Vartika's eyes lit up with genuine warmth. "Not at all, Paras! How's your day going so far?"

Paras's smile widened. "It's been great, especially with all this positive energy around. Your vibe is infectious."

Vartika's cheeks flushed with a hint of bashful appreciation. "Positive energy is my middle name! Well, not really, but you get the idea. How about you? Enjoying the new office life?"

Paras's gaze sparkled with enthusiasm. "Absolutely! It feels like a breath of fresh air, a new chapter, you know? And meeting awesome colleagues like you makes it even better."

Vartika's eyes softened with gratitude. "Flattery will get you everywhere, Paras. But seriously, it's nice to have a friendly face around. What do you think of the project we're working on?"

Paras's excitement was palpable. "I'm excited about it! I think our dynamic duo can create something fantastic together. What's your secret to bringing so much energy to the workplace?"

Vartika's laughter bubbled forth, accompanied by a twinkle in her eye. "Oh, it's no secret just a mix of passion, coffee, and a dash of good company. By the way, do you have any hidden talents or hobbies I should know about?"

Paras's expression softened, revealing a glimpse of vulnerability. "Well, I'm not sure about hidden talents, but I'm into reading and writing poetry. It's my way of escaping reality for a bit."

Vartika's curiosity was piqued. "Poetry? That's intriguing! You'll have to share some with me sometime. Maybe we can turn our project meetings into a creative space."

Paras's heart skipped a beat at the thought of sharing his poetry with Vartika. "I'd like that, Vartika. Who knew an internship could bring such interesting twists?"

Vartika's smile mirrored his own, tinged with a sense of wonder. "Life is full of surprises, Paras. Here's to unexpected threads weaving into our journey."

Destiny, in its subtle orchestration, aligned their paths even further as they collaborated on a project. Beyond Vartika's lively exterior, Paras discovered layers of depth and substance that intrigued him. The unfolding chapters of his life took an unforeseen turn, and he, once tethered to the memories of the past, found himself captivated by the unexpected charm of the present. Her intelligence and wit matched her outward charm, and their teamwork was seamless. It wasn't long before their professional conversations evolved into personal discussions, and they decided to exchange numbers. The transition from colleagues to friends felt effortless, and before Paras knew it, they were making plans to hang out outside of work.

Paras: Hey! have you tried the coffee from the new place down the street? It's supposed to be amazing.

Vartika's eyes sparkled with excitement. "Oh, really? I'm always up for good coffee. Maybe we should check it out together sometime."

Paras grinned; his anticipation evident. "That sounds like a plan. I could use some expert guidance on navigating the coffee menu."

Vartika chuckled, adopting a mock serious expression. "Expert guidance? Well, I do take my coffee choices very seriously. Consider me your coffee connoisseur."

Paras couldn't help but laugh. "Lucky me. I always appreciate someone with refined tastes. By the way, did you know they have this special blend that's supposed to be a game-changer?"

Vartika's eyebrows lifted in intrigue. "A game-changer, huh? Well, you've definitely piqued my interest. When are we embarking on this coffee adventure?"

Paras's eyes gleamed with mischief. "How about tomorrow after work? We can be each other's taste-testers and rate the coffee on our very official scale."

Vartika threw her head back in laughter. "Official coffee critics it is then. Tomorrow it is!"

Vartika's flirtatious behavior, leaning into his conversations and showing genuine interest in his hobbies and passions, didn't go unnoticed. Paras couldn't help but be flattered by her attention, finding himself increasingly drawn to her He had his reservations, though. He didn't want to jump into a new relationship hastily, fearing that he might just be rebounding from his past. Yet, as he spent more time with Vartika, he realized that his feelings for her were growing beyond just friendship. Their connection felt natural and easy, like they had known each other for much longer. Their first official date was a testament to their compatibility. They chose a trendy restaurant in the heart of the city, where they spent the evening engrossed in conversation, laughter, and shared interests. Paras was captivated by Vartika's charm and the depth of their discussions. It was evident that there was something special between them.

Vartika approached Paras with a warm smile. "Hey, Paras, we've been working really hard lately. How about we take a break and grab dinner tonight? My treat!"

Paras, pleasantly surprised by the invitation, smiled back. "Dinner sounds great, Vartika. I'd love to."

Later that evening, they found themselves at a trendy restaurant in the heart of the city. The ambiance was perfect—soft lighting, faint music in the background, and a menu that promised a culinary delight. As they delved into conversation, Paras discovered a genuine connection with Vartika. The topics flowed effortlessly, and their laughter felt natural and unforced. Suddenly, Vartika, her eyes sparkling with enthusiasm, turned to Paras. "You know, Paras, we really do make a great team. Working together has been such a fantastic experience."

Paras nodded, a smile playing on his lips. "Absolutely, Vartika. I couldn't have asked for a better partner on this project."

Vartika, leaning in a bit, added, "I mean, it's rare to find someone you click with so well, both professionally and personally."

Paras, feeling a flutter of excitement, replied, "I totally agree. It's been really refreshing working with you, and getting to know you outside of work has been even better."

Vartika chuckled, "I've been thinking... what if we tried hanging out more, outside of work? You know, just to see where things go."

Paras, taken aback but intrigued, looked at her with a mix of curiosity and delight. "Wait, are you saying what I think you're saying?"

Vartika grinned, "Yeah, I guess I am. How about we give 'us' a shot? I mean, why not see if there's more to this partnership than just office stuff?"

Paras, feeling his heart race with a blend of excitement and joy, smiled, "Vartika, I'd really like that. Let's do it. Let's see where this takes us."

But as their relationship progressed, Paras found himself at a crossroads as the dynamics of his relationship with Vartika continued to unfold. The initial enchantment that drew him to her was now tainted with the toxicity that had begun to surface. The fiery passion he mistook for intensity now revealed a more challenging side of Vartika. The signs were undeniable. Her temper, once thought of as a manifestation of passion, now appeared more like a destructive force. Minor issues triggered disproportionate reactions, leading to hurtful arguments that left Paras emotionally drained. Despite the red flags, Paras clung to the hope that every relationship faced challenges. He convinced himself that patience and understanding were essential ingredients in navigating the complexities of love. Vartika's occasional flirtation and the seemingly genuine care she displayed during moments of vulnerability created a conflicting emotional landscape for Paras. However, a persistent pattern of manipulation began to emerge. Vartika employed emotional tactics to influence Paras's decisions, from canceling plans with friends to meet her demands.

Paras, with a hopeful tone, "Hey, Vartika, I was thinking of catching up with my friends this Saturday. It's been a while, and I miss spending time with them."

Vartika, smiling warmly, "Oh, Paras, that sounds nice, but I was really hoping we could have a cozy weekend together. You know, just the two of us. I've been feeling a bit low, and your company always lifts my spirits."

Paras, torn between conflicting commitments, "Well, we can still spend time together on Sunday. I just promised my friends I'd join them, and I don't want to cancel on them again."

Vartika, playfully pouting her lips, "I thought you cared about me. I'm going through a rough time, and you're choosing your friends over me? I thought I could count on you."

Paras, feeling a pang of guilt, "No, Vartika, it's not that I don't care about you. It's just that I can't keep canceling plans with my friends. They're important to me too. I've had to bail on them for you the last three times."

Vartika, softening her tone, "I just thought you understood

how much I need you right now. But if your friends are more important, then go ahead. Do what makes you happy."

Paras, feeling a bit manipulated, "It's not about choosing between you and my friends. I just want to find a balance."

Paras, calling in front of Vartika, "Hey, I know I promised to hang out on Saturday, but something came up. Can we reschedule for next weekend?"

Friends, expressing disappointment, "Again, Paras? You've been canceling plans quite a bit lately."

Paras, apologetic, "Yeah, I know, and I'm really sorry about that. It's just... Vartika needed me, and I couldn't say no."

Friends, expressing concern, "Paras, I get that relationships are important, but don't forget about your friends. We're here for you too."

Paras, torn between loyalty and the desire to be fair, "I know, and I appreciate that. It's just, you know…!"

He ended the call, the frustration lingered. He felt that he was caught in a web of conflicting priorities. This incident marked another step in realizing that the dynamics with Vartika might be more toxic than he initially acknowledged.

As the unsettling reality of their relationship dawned on Paras, he grappled with the conflicting emotions within him. The allure of Vartika's flirtatious charm clashed with the toxicity that had crept into their connection. Paras acknowledged a fundamental truth: he deserved a relationship founded on mutual respect, trust, and genuine care. The boundaries of a healthy partnership had blurred, and Paras couldn't ignore the toll it took on his emotional well-being. He realized that while Vartika's flirtatious behavior might be momentarily appealing, it didn't excuse the toxic patterns that were emerging. It was a challenging realization, forcing Paras to confront the stark contrast between the surface-level attraction and the deeper, more significant aspects of a fulfilling relationship. With determination, Paras decided to prioritize his own well-being. He understood that love shouldn't come at the cost of emotional turmoil and constant tension. He sought a relationship that uplifted him, provided genuine support, and allowed him to thrive as an individual. One day Vartika's temper flared up over a seemingly trivial disagreement, and Paras felt the weight of her anger directed at him.

Vartika, expressing frustration, "I can't believe you're so insensitive, Paras! You never understand how I feel."

Paras, trying to diffuse the tension, "Vartika, let's not blow this out of proportion. We can talk about it calmly."

Vartika, feeling overlooked, "You always take her side, don't you? Myra, Myra, Myra! You care more about her than you care about me!"

Paras, trying to explain, "Vartika, it's not about taking sides. Myra is my best friend, and she's important to me, just like you are. Let's not turn this into a competition."

Vartika, feeling neglected, "You're always defending her. Maybe you should just be with her instead!"

Paras, feeling unfairly accused, "That's not fair, Vartika. This is about us, not Myra. Let's find a way to communicate without bringing others into it."

Vartika, expressing her needs, "Well, maybe if you paid more attention to me, we wouldn't have these issues."

Paras, willing to address the problem, "Okay, let's talk about us then. What can we do to make our relationship better? How can we avoid these arguments?"

Vartika, expressing her desire, "I just want you to prioritize me over others."

Paras, showing understanding, "I care about you, Vartika. Let's work on understanding each other better, but we shouldn't drag others into our problems, right?"

The tough decision to distance himself from Vartika became a step towards reclaiming his own happiness and pursuing a connection that aligned with his values and aspirations. Paras was ready to embark on a journey toward a healthier, more fulfilling relationship, free from the shadows of toxicity that had eclipsed his initial feelings of love.

Paras, trying to plan a nice weekend, "Hey, I was thinking we could go out to that new Italian place this weekend. What do you think?"

Vartika, expressing fatigue, "Ugh, I don't know. I'm just so tired of going out to eat all the time. Can't we just stay in and watch a movie?"

Paras, accommodating, "Sure, that sounds like a good idea too. What do you want to watch?"

Vartika, indifferent, "I don't care, whatever you want. But I better not fall asleep this time, or you'll be in trouble."

Paras, expressing concern, "Don't worry, I'll keep you awake. Hey, can I ask you something?"

Vartika, open to discussion, "Sure, what's up?"

Paras, expressing his feelings, "I feel like sometimes you get really angry with me over small things. Is everything okay?"

Vartika, sharing her frustration, "You just don't get it, do you? You're always so distant and aloof. I just want you to be more present with me."

Paras, showing willingness to change, "I'm sorry if I've been distant. I'll try to be more present. But can we talk about the way you've been treating me lately? It feels like you're always angry with me."

Vartika, frustrated, "Here we go again. You..."

Paras, confused, "What do you mean?"

Vartika, "You're always so negative about everything. It's exhausting."

Paras, defending his perspective, "I'm not negative. I just don't like to get my hopes up too high."

Vartika, showing concern, "That's the problem. You never let yourself be happy. You're always waiting for the other shoe to drop."

Paras, feeling attacked, "Well, maybe if you stopped trying to change me all the time, we wouldn't be arguing like this."

Vartika, expressing her intention, "I'm not trying to change you. I just want you to be happy."

Paras, attempting to diffuse the tension, "Look, can we just forget about this argument and enjoy the rest of our date?"

Vartika, agreeing, "Sure, let's do that."

Despite the argument, the rest of the date went well. Paras and Vartika had a nice time together, but he felt that something was off. Over the next few weeks, Vartika became increasingly demanding and controlling, often picking fights with Paras over small things. Eventually, Paras realized that he had made a mistake by getting involved with her. Paras started to feel suffocated by the relationship, and he realized that he wasn't happy anymore. He tried to talk to Vartika about their issues, but she would always turn it around on him, making him feel like he was the problem.

Paras found himself caught in the whirlwind of emotions as his relationship with Vartika progressed. While there were moments of joy and connection, he couldn't ignore the growing toxicity that was seeping into their interactions. As his concerns deepened, he decided to confide in Myra, his trusted friend who had been there through all of life's ups and downs.

As he poured his heart out to Myra in the cozy ambiance of their favorite coffee shop, he felt a sense of relief, unburdening the weight that had been silently pressing on him. Myra's empathetic demeanor provided a safe space for him to unravel the complexities of his relationship with

Vartika. He started from the beginning, narrating the story of how Vartika's vibrant personality had drawn him in, making each interaction a highlight of his day. Myra's knowing smiles and encouraging nods reassured Paras that he was in a judgment-free zone. As the story unfolded, from the enchanting first date to the escalating conflicts, Paras painted a vivid picture of the emotional rollercoaster he found himself on. Myra's expressions mirrored the ebb and flow of Paras's narrative, a testament to her ability to empathize with the intricacies of his emotions.

"So, Myra," Paras sighed, "I don't know what to do. On one hand, Vartika and I have this undeniable connection. She's so charming, and our conversations just flow effortlessly. But on the other hand, her temper and manipulative behavior are starting to wear me down."

Myra leaned forward, her expression a mix of concern and empathy. "Paras, it's important to pay attention to those red flags. No relationship should come at the cost of your emotional well-being."

Paras nodded; his gaze fixed on the table. "I know you're right. It's just that she can be so sweet and flirtatious, and those moments make me second-guess my doubts. But then, she can turn around and get furious over the smallest things."

Myra placed a reassuring hand on Paras's arm. "It sounds like you're experiencing some emotional manipulation, Paras. Healthy relationships are built on communication, trust, and respect. If those elements are missing and you're constantly walking on eggshells, it might be time to reevaluate things."

Paras let out a heavy sigh. "I guess I've been afraid to admit it to myself. I don't want to end up in another unhealthy relationship like I did with Akshi."

Myra smiled warmly. "Learning from past experiences is a sign of growth, Paras. You deserve happiness and a relationship where you're valued for who you are."

Paras looked up, meeting Myra's eyes. "You've always been there for me, Myra. Your perspective is so clear, and I appreciate your honesty."

Myra squeezed his arm gently. "Paras just trust your instincts and prioritize your own well-being. Whether it's with Vartika or someone else, I just want to see you happy."

He felt a sense of clarity he hadn't experienced in a while. Myra's words had resonated deeply, reminding him of his worth and the importance of being in a healthy relationship. After this heart-to-heart conversation with Myra, Paras was determined to salvage his relationship with Vartika. He believed that communication and understanding could bridge the gap that had been growing between them. He planned a thoughtful evening, hoping to address their issues and reignite the spark they had once shared.

Paras invited Vartika to a cozy, candlelit dinner at a charming restaurant. He had prepared himself mentally to approach the conversation with empathy and patience. As they sat down, Vartika seemed to be in a pleasant mood, smiling and chatting animatedly. Paras couldn't help but feel a glimmer of hope that this might mark a positive turning point for them. As they delved into their meal, Paras gently broached the topic he had been wanting to discuss. "Vartika, there's something on my mind that I think we need to address. I really care about us, and I believe that open communication is key."

Vartika looked at him, her expression neutral. "Sure, go ahead."

Paras took a deep breath. "I've noticed that sometimes our interactions become tense, and there are instances where misunderstandings lead to arguments. I want us to work through these challenges together, so we can grow as a couple."

Vartika's response was unexpectedly dismissive. "Paras, it's just how I am. If you can't handle it, maybe we're not right for each other."

Paras was taken aback by her lack of willingness to engage. He had hoped for a constructive dialogue, but it seemed that Vartika was resistant to acknowledging the issues. He tried to keep his calm. "I want to understand you better, Vartika. Is there something that triggers these reactions? Can we find a way to work through them?"

Vartika's demeanor shifted, her tone sharper. "Look, Paras, this is who I am. I'm not going to change just to fit into some 'perfect' relationship mold. Take it or leave it."

Paras felt a mix of frustration and disappointment. He had genuinely wanted to address their problems and find a way forward, but it seemed that Vartika was not interested in making any changes. As the evening progressed, Paras realized that his efforts were in vain. The conversation remained strained, and he couldn't shake the feeling that they were stuck in a loop of unhealthy dynamics.

In the days that followed, Paras found himself constantly replaying the unsuccessful dinner conversation with Vartika. The weight of the situation grew heavier on his mind with each passing day. Myra's words echoed in his ears, reminding him that a healthy relationship required both partners to be willing to work together. One evening, as he sat in his living room, his phone buzzed with a message from Vartika. His heart skipped a beat as he read her words, "Hey Paras, how have you been?" Despite the apprehension, he knew it was time to address the elephant in the room.

Paras took a deep breath, his fingers slightly trembling as he typed a response, "Hi Vartika, I've been doing some thinking, and I believe we need to have an honest conversation."

Vartika's reply was almost instantaneous, "What's there to talk about? If you can't handle me as I am, then maybe we're not meant to be."

Paras felt a mixture of frustration and determination. He knew that he needed to express his feelings and stand up for what he believed in. He began typing, his words careful yet firm, "Vartika, I care about you a lot, but I also care about myself and my emotional well-being. A healthy relationship is about communication, understanding, and growth. It's not about changing who we are, but it's about being open to compromise and finding common ground."

There was a brief pause before Vartika replied, "I won't change who I am just to fit into your idea of a 'perfect' relationship."

Paras took a moment to collect his thoughts before responding, "Vartika, I'm not asking you to change who you are. I'm asking for mutual respect and a willingness to work through challenges together. I believe we both deserve that."

The conversation continued, their messages going back and forth. Paras poured his heart into his responses, hoping to convey his feelings and concerns without being confrontational. However, Vartika remained defensive, holding onto her stance that she shouldn't have to change for anyone. As the conversation reached a point of impasse, Paras realized that he had done all he could. He knew that he deserved a relationship built on a strong foundation of understanding and compromise. With a heavy heart, he typed his final message, "Vartika, I need to prioritize my emotional well-being. I want us both to be happy, even if it means going our separate ways."

Vartika's reply was swift and cutting, "Fine, go ahead and leave. You'll never find someone who 'fits' your mold."

As Paras pressed the end call button on his phone, the silence that enveloped his living room was both sad and liberating. A mixture of sadness and relief coursed through him, echoing the complexity of untangling oneself from a toxic relationship. In that quiet space, Paras couldn't deny the freedom that began to unfold within him. It was as if he had lifted a weight off his shoulders, shedding the burden of a relationship that had veered far from the path of health and happiness.

Yet, as he reflected on the situation, Paras found himself caught in a paradox. Walking away from the toxic relationship brought a relief, but it also led him to confront the unsettling realization that he might have jumped from one unhealthy situation to another. The echoes of toxicity lingered, leaving Paras in a state of introspection, questioning the patterns that had led him from one challenging relationship to the next. He was disappointed that his rebound relationship had turned out to be a disaster, but he knew that he had learned valuable lessons about what he wanted and didn't want in a partner. Paras spent the next few days feeling down and defeated. He had thought that he had finally moved on from Akshi and found someone new, but it seemed like history was repeating itself. He couldn't help but feel frustrated that his efforts to make things work with Vartika had come to an end. As Paras sat with Myra, sharing his feelings and the details of his recent separation, his phone suddenly buzzed. He glanced at the screen and was surprised to see Vartika's name flashing on it. His heart skipped a beat, a mix of emotions swirling within him - surprise, curiosity, and a touch of anxiety.

Myra noticed the change in his expression. "Who's calling?"

Paras hesitated for a moment, contemplating whether to answer the call or not. Finally, he sighed and answered, "It's Vartika."

Myra raised an eyebrow. "Do you want to take the call?"

Paras shrugged; his expression conflicted. "I'm not sure. Maybe I should just let it go."

Myra nodded understandingly. "Do what feels right for you. If you're not ready to talk, it's okay."

The call ended, and Paras let out a deep breath. "I think I'll listen to what she has to say. Maybe closure will help me move on."

Myra patted his shoulder. "Just remember, Paras, you deserve happiness and a healthy relationship. Don't settle for less."

With a determined nod, Paras returned the call. Vartika's voice sounded uncertain on the other end. "Paras, I... I know you said what you needed to say, but can we talk."

Her tone was different from what he had expected – it was softer, more subdued.

Paras exchanged a puzzled glance with Myra before responding cautiously, "Hi, Vartika. Is everything okay?"

There was a brief pause before Vartika spoke again. "I... I've been doing some thinking. And I wanted to talk to you."

Paras's heart skipped a beat. He hadn't anticipated this turn of events. "Sure, Vartika. What did you want to talk about?"

"I've been reflecting on our conversation," Vartika began, her voice carrying a hint of vulnerability. "And I realize that maybe I haven't been as open to compromise as I should have been."

Paras listened intently, feeling a mixture of surprise and cautious hope. This was a side of Vartika he hadn't seen before.

"I know that I can be stubborn and quick to anger," Vartika continued. "But I also care about you, Paras. And I don't want to lose what we had because of my own shortcomings."

Paras felt a wave of conflicting emotions wash over him – surprise, hope, and a touch of skepticism. He exchanged a meaningful look with Myra, who offered an encouraging nod.

"Vartika, I appreciate your honesty," Paras replied, his voice sincere. "But for us to move forward, there needs to be genuine change. We both deserve a healthy relationship, one where we can communicate and grow together.

There was a moment of silence before Vartika spoke again, her voice determined. "I'm willing to work on myself, Paras. I want to try to make things right between us."

She was crying and apologizing for the way she had treated him, saying that she realized too late how much he had meant to her. Paras felt a glimmer of hope that things could work out between them.

On the other hand, he couldn't forget the pain and toxicity that had plagued their relationship. Mayra, who was sitting next to him, noticed the change in Paras' expression and leaned in to listen.

"I don't know, Vartika," Paras said hesitantly. "I need some time to think about this. I don't want to rush into anything."

Vartika nodded, tears still streaming down her face. "I understand, Paras. Please just know that I'm truly sorry and that I love you."

He knew he had a lot to think about before talking to Vartika the next day. Paras called Vartika the next day at the park where they used to go. As he walked to the park the next day, he felt mix of anticipation and anxiety. He knew that this conversation with Vartika was crucial, and he wanted to approach it with honesty and clarity.

He saw Vartika waiting at their usual spot, a flood of memories rushed back the laughter, the conversations, and the good times they had shared. But he also reminded himself of the challenges and struggles they had faced

"Hey Vartika," he greeted her, his voice warm yet cautious.

"Hi paras," Vartika replied, her eyes reflecting a mix of emotions.

They both settled on a bench, and for a moment, there was a comfortable silence. Paras took a deep breath, gathering his thoughts before he spoke.

"I really appreciate your apology, Vartika," he began, looking at her earnestly. "It takes courage to admit one's mistakes, and I respect that."

Vartika nodded, her expression a blend of understanding and regret.

"But I've been doing a lot of thinking," Paras continued, his tone gentle but firm. "And I've come to realize that our relationship was more toxic than I allowed myself to believe. I believe that we both need to move forward separately."

Vartika's eyes welled up with tears, and Paras felt a twinge of pain in his chest. He didn't want to hurt her, but he knew that staying in a relationship that wasn't healthy wouldn't be fair to either of them.

"I'm not saying this to hurt you," Paras added, his voice

softening. "I'm saying it because I think it's the best decision for both of us."

Vartika wiped away a tear, her gaze meeting his. "I understand, Paras. And I appreciate your honesty."

Paras reached out and placed a reassuring hand on her shoulder. "Vartika, we both deserve to be in relationships where we can grow and support each other. I truly hope you find that."

Vartika managed a small smile through her tears. "Thank you, Paras. I really do wish you all the best too."

As they sat in silence for a moment, Paras felt a mix of emotions – sadness for the end of a chapter, but also a sense of relief and liberation.

He knew that he had made the right decision for his own well-being, and he hoped that Vartika would also find the path to healing and personal growth.

After a while, they both stood up. Paras looked at Vartika one last time and they both hugged.

"Take care, Vartika," he said softly.

"You too, Paras," Vartika replied, her voice tinged with emotion.

As he walked away from the park, he felt a weight lift off his shoulders. He knew that he had made a difficult but necessary choice, and he was finally free to move forward without the weight of a toxic relationship holding him back. Paras had learned an invaluable lesson from his experience with Vartika

- the rebound may offer temporary solace to a broken heart, but it should never come at the expense of one's well-being.

In matters of the heart, it's crucial to heed our inner voice and not be swayed by temporary comfort, especially when it leads to toxicity and emotional turmoil. For true love to thrive, it requires a foundation of mutual respect, understanding, and healthy communication. So let us never forget the importance of valuing ourselves and listening to our intuition in matters of the heart.

"Sometimes, the rebound can be a temporary fix to a broken heart, but it's important to listen to our intuition and not settle for toxicity in the name of love."

"Sometimes, the path to true love isn't a straight line. We may encounter detours, roadblocks, and unexpected turns along the way. But it's important to keep an open heart, to learn from our past mistakes, and to trust in the journey. Because in the end, the destination is worth it - whether it leads us back to a lost love or to someone new who will cherish our hearts."

<u>Missing Out</u>

"Missing out is not just about the things we didn't do or the experiences we didn't have. It's about the people we didn't let into our lives, the connections we didn't embrace, and the love we didn't allow ourselves to feel. In the pursuit of independence, we sometimes forget the power of vulnerability and the beauty of shared experiences. Don't let the fear of missing out on genuine connections rob you of the joy that comes from truly knowing and being known by others."

As the seasons cast their subtle transformations upon the world, an unnoticed shift began to weave its presence into the tapestry of Akshi's life. Unfurling gradually, like the petals of a delicate bloom, it made itself known through a faint but persistent feeling of absence. At first, Akshi found herself unable to pinpoint the source of this subtle void, an intangible yearning that lingered in the corners of her daily existence. Days melded into weeks, and weeks into months, and the realization dawned on her like the soft glow of dawn she was missing someone. For Akshi, a person who had always prided herself on self-sufficiency and resilience, this acknowledgment came as a quiet revelation. She had navigated life with an air of confidence, drawing happiness from within and never relying on external factors to define her sense of fulfillment. Yet, in the quiet moments when the world around her hushed into stillness, Akshi felt the echo of a companion absent. It wasn't a loud void, but a persistent whisper that nudged at the edges of her consciousness. One evening, seated by her window, curtains gently dancing in tandem with a breeze, Akshi found herself facing the hollowness within. The room's silence mirrored the quieter spaces of her heart, and her thoughts embarked on a reflective journey through time.

In her memories, she retraced the steps that led to this unspoken void. The vibrant conversations that once painted her days with hues of joy, the easy camaraderie that filled the silences between words, and the understanding that had flowed effortlessly between her and Paras all of it gained a newfound significance as she pondered upon the solitude that had nestled itself into her life, subtly and without conscious realization.

She found herself unraveling layers of emotions, each revelation casting a sad light on the depth of her feelings for Paras. She delved into the reservoir of memories, retrieving snippets of shared laughter, intimate conversations, and the nuanced understanding that had woven itself seamlessly into the fabric of their connection. "Why do I feel this ache deep within me? I've always prided myself on my independence and self-reliance. But lately, I can't shake off the longing for Paras's presence."

She paused, contemplating the reasons behind her yearning.

"Perhaps it's his infectious laughter, the way he effortlessly brings joy into my life. I miss the sound of our laughter, filling the room with warmth and mirth."

She sighed, recognizing another aspect of her emotions. "Paras has this remarkable ability to truly listen. He sees through the facade of strength I put up for the world. He understands me in ways that no one else does. I miss his comforting presence, the solace I find in his unwavering support."

Her thoughts wandered further, unraveling her newfound understanding.

"I used to think that needing someone meant weakness, but I've come to realize that it's not. It's a testament to the connection we share, the bond that transcends superficial expectations. It's okay to admit that I need him in my life."

She paused, her heart growing heavier with each passing realization.

"Paras's presence has taught me the beauty of genuine connections. It's not just about independence; it's about finding those who truly understand and accept us, flaws and all. And he does."

Her contemplation shifted, her mind racing with a newfound determination.

"I need to express my gratitude to Paras, to let him know how much his presence means to me. I want to cherish our friendship, nurture it with the care and attention it deserves. It's time to embrace the depth of my feelings and take the leap towards a richer connection."

She truly understood the impact he had on her life. The days seemed less vibrant, and the laughter that once echoed through her days seemed to fade away. She longed for their conversations, their shared jokes, and the sense of comfort she felt when he was around. During this time of separation, Akshi discovered something about herself that she had kept hidden from others. Beneath her confident exterior, there was a longing for connection, and a genuine need for companionship. In her quiet moments of reflection, Akshi thought back to the moments she had spent with Paras. She remembered his warmth, his genuine care, and the way he effortlessly made her feel valued. As the night deepened, Akshi's room became a sanctuary for introspection. Paras had become a witness to a side of her that few others had seen, a side she herself had grappled with acknowledging.

The realization brought forth a mixture of emotions, gratitude for Paras's understanding and a subtle regret for not fully appreciating it in the past. Lying on her bed, thoughts swirled like a tempest within her. She recognized the need to confide in someone who truly understood her, someone who had been a steadfast pillar of support. Without hesitation, she reached for her phone and dialed Vishaka's number, her lifelong best friend. In the upcoming conversation, Akshi would share the complexities of her emotions, the newfound understanding of her weekness, and the longing for a connection that had become an integral part of her existence.

With a few rings, Vishaka's warm voice filled the line. "Hey, Akshi! What's going on? It's been a while since we caught up."

Akshi took a moment to steady her emotions before speaking. "Hey, Vishaka. I really need to talk. It's about Paras."

Vishaka's tone shifted, becoming more attentive. "Of course, Akshi. You know you can always talk to me. What's on your mind?"

Taking a deep breath, Akshi decided to open up to Vishaka, her lifelong close friend. She began unraveling the tapestry of her emotions, articulating the newfound realization of Paras's significance in her life and the void that had gradually taken shape in his absence. The words flowed, carrying with them the weight of vulnerability and a sense of longing she had kept hidden. As she shared her conflicting thoughts with Vishaka, she expressed the turmoil within her the desire to bring Paras back into her life, to reclaim the shared laughter and comfort, and yet, the fear that such a request might alter the delicate balance of their existing dynamics. The uncertainty of navigating the complexities of emotions lay bare in her words.

Vishaka, a seasoned listener and a pillar of support, absorbed Akshi's narrative with unwavering attention. She created a safe space for Akshi to voice her feelings, allowing the emotions to spill forth without judgment. The room, though physically empty, resonated with the echoes of a conversation that transcended the ordinary. When Akshi's words finally ceased, the room held a lingering hush, awaiting Vishaka's response. With an understanding tone, Vishaka prepared to offer insights and guidance to navigate the intricate maze of emotions that Akshi found herself entangled in.

"Akshi, it's clear that Paras has made a deep impact on your life. It's natural to miss someone who has touched your heart and mind. True connections are rare and precious; they shape us in ways we often don't anticipate."

Akshi nodded, appreciating Vishaka's perspective. "But Vishaka, I'm scared. I don't want to jeopardize our friendship or make things awkward. What if expressing my feelings ruins what we have?"

Vishaka's response was thoughtful. "I understand your concerns, Akshi. But remember, genuine friendships thrive on honesty and open dialogue. It might be worth discussing your feelings with Paras. He's shown you consistent support, and there's a possibility he feels the same way. At the very least, he can offer you some clarity."

Akshi contemplated Vishaka's words, realizing that fear had been holding her back. Deep down, she knew that transparency was vital to maintaining the authenticity of their connection.

"You're right, Vishaka. I should be honest with Paras and share my feelings with him. I don't want to live with regrets or the uncertainty of 'what if.' Our friendship can withstand any outcome."

Vishaka's encouragement resonated deeply with Akshi. "That's the spirit, Akshi! Regardless of what happens, remember that you're not alone. I'll be here for you every step of the way. Trust yourself, trust Paras, and trust the bond you share."

In the midst of their conversation, Vishaka added a thoughtful perspective. "You know, Akshi, I think it's important to acknowledge that what you did back then – leaving Paras isolated and ignoring his emotions – wasn't fair to him. It's commendable that you're willing to face this head-on now."

Akshi sighed, recognizing the truth in Vishaka's words. "You're right, Vishaka. I need to make amends for that too. He deserved better."

As they continued the conversation, her thoughts delved deeper into the past. She realized that her actions had not only caused her to lose a genuine person from her life but had also prevented her from fully embracing a chance at love.

Tears welled up in Akshi's eyes as she admitted, "Vishaka, I can't believe how blind I was back then. I treated him so unfairly, shutting him out and not even giving him a chance to express his feelings. I was so afraid of my own emotions that I hurt him in the process."

Vishaka's voice softened with empathy. "It's never too late to make things right, Akshi. What's important is that you're recognizing your mistakes and taking responsibility for them. Sometimes, we learn from our missteps and grow into better versions of ourselves."

Akshi wiped away a tear, her heart heavy with regret. "I wish I could go back in time and change things. He deserved to be treated with kindness and respect, not pushed away like that."

Vishaka offered a reassuring perspective. "Remember, Akshi, growth comes from acknowledging our past mistakes and working to rectify them. Maybe it's time to reach out to Paras and have an honest conversation about your feelings – both then and now."

Akshi took a deep breath, considering Vishaka's words. "You're right, Vishaka. I owe it to him and myself to clear the air. Whether we end up together or not, I need to apologize for my past behavior and let him know how much I value his presence in my life."

She gathered her thoughts and summoned the courage to take the first step towards making amends. One evening, she picked up her phone and texted Paras. It was a message she had spent hours drafting and redrafting, ensuring that every word conveyed the sincerity of her intentions.

"Paras," she started, her fingertips hovering over the screen, a subtle tremble revealing the vulnerability beneath her usually composed exterior. "I hope this message reaches you in a moment of understanding. It's been too long, and I can imagine the surprise of seeing my name on your screen. The passage of time has been a companion to my reflections on our shared history. And in these moments of introspection, the weight of my actions has become painfully clear. I mistreated you, unfairly and thoughtlessly, causing you pain. For that, I carry a profound and sincere apology."

As the send button stared back at her, Akshi hesitated for a moment before finally pressing it. The message was sent, and she felt a mix of anxiety and anticipation swirling within her. On the other side of town, Paras's phone lit up with a notification his curiosity mingled with surprise at the sight of Akshi's name. Months had passed since their last interaction, and the unexpected message stirred a whirlwind of emotions within him. With cautious anticipation, Paras opened the message, his eyes scanning the words that spilled across the screen. The weight of Akshi's apology resonated with him, touching the depths of emotions that time had failed to erase. Her sincerity, laid bare in the text, bridged the temporal gap between their last encounter and the present moment. Paras found himself caught in the ebb and flow of nostalgia, memories of their shared past intertwining with the strides he had taken to move forward in his life. He had moved forward in his life, focusing on his own growth and well-being. But the memories of his time with Akshi still lingered, and her message stirred a nostalgia and reflection within him. After taking some time to compose his thoughts, Paras replied to Akshi's message. "Hi Akshi, thank you for reaching out. Your apology means a lot to me, and I appreciate your honesty. I've also had time to reflect on everything. It's good to hear from you. What's on your mind?"

As the conversation continued, Akshi and Paras exchanged updates on their lives, sharing snippets of their individual journeys over the past few months. Akshi was relieved by Paras's receptive and understanding tone, which helped ease the tension that had built up in her mind. Finally, after some back-and-forth, Akshi mustered the courage to address the main reason for her message.

"Paras, I know we both have our own lives now, and I respect that. But I can't ignore how much I value the bond we shared. Would you be open to meeting sometime? I'd really like to talk face-to-face. I'll be returning from college next week."

Paras read the message, his thoughts racing as he considered the proposition. He knew that meeting with Akshi could potentially bring up a flood of emotions and memories. But he also acknowledged that closure was important for both of them.

Taking a deep breath, Paras typed his response. "Akshi, I think a face-to-face conversation could be a good idea. Let's meet. We can decide on a time and place that works for both of us."

Akshi knew that reaching out to Paras and sharing her feelings might be a leap into the unknown, but she also understood that taking risks was sometimes necessary to find true happiness. She realized that life was too short to hide behind fear and that embracing vulnerability was the only way to truly experience the richness of human connections.

And so, armed with courage and guided by the unwavering support of her best friend, Akshi set forth on a journey to express her emotions to Paras, knowing that no matter the outcome, she had taken a step towards embracing her true self and the potential for a deeper connection with someone she cared deeply about.

The Closure Conversation

"You can't start the next chapter of your life if you keep re-reading the last one."

Paras had finally made peace with his past relationships, but there was still one loose end that needed tying up. He had never fully addressed the issues with Akshi and he knew it was time to have a closure conversation with her. He had moved on from his feelings for her, but he didn't want to leave any lingering questions or doubts.

The meet up day arrived, and Paras sitting on a bench at the park, He had chosen a spot that held no particular memories for them, a neutral ground for their conversation. He felt nervous, as he gazed around, taking in the familiar sights of the park, waiting for Akshi to arrive, his thoughts drifted back to the past reflecting on the journey that had led him to this moment. Paras, it's been a long road, he thought. From the highs of meeting Akshi to the depths of heartbreak. Funny how life twists and turns.

Back then, you thought Akshi was the one, the person who would be by your side no matter what. You were willing to do anything for her, to sacrifice your own well-being for her happiness. But you've learned that a healthy relationship is built on mutual support. When Akshi ended things and moved on, it shattered you. You questioned your worth, wondered if there was something inherently wrong with you. But that pain also pushed you to explore who you are outside of a relationship. You poured yourself into your work, your hobbies, and your friendships. You rebuilt your self-esteem and realized that your value isn't determined by someone else's opinion. And then there was Vartika someone who seemed promising at first, but whose behavior raised red flags. You were strong enough to recognize the signs of toxicity and walk away, even if it was hard. It was a tough decision, but it showed how far you've come in understanding your own worth. Now, you're here, waiting to have a closure conversation with Akshi. It's a step towards healing, towards letting go of any lingering doubts or what-ifs. You're not the same person you were when you first met her, and that's a good thing. You've learned that true growth comes from acknowledging your mistakes and taking responsibility for them. No matter what happens in this conversation, Paras, remember that you're doing it for yourself. You're seeking closure not because you still have feelings for Akshi, but because you want to put the past behind you.

It's time to fully embrace the present and the future that lies ahead. Paras's internal monologue was interrupted as he saw Akshi approaching.

The park bench, a silent witness to countless conversations, now hosted the reunion of Paras and Akshi. As they exchanged pleasantries, a palpable tension hung in the air, a silent acknowledgment of the weighty conversation awaiting them. They settled into their seats, facing each other, the unspoken words echoing louder than the ones they were about to share. Paras, breaking the silence, began to speak. His voice, a blend of introspection and vulnerability, carried the weight of the untold stories that lingered between them. Akshi listened intently, her gaze unwavering, absorbing the nuances of his emotions.

"Paras, I'm glad you reached out. I've been meaning to talk to you too," Akshi said, breaking the silence.

For a few moments, they sat in silence, both of them lost in thought. Paras felt a weight lifting off his shoulders, as though a burden that he had been carrying for months was finally being lifted. The park seemed to cocoon them in a quiet bubble as they continued their conversation. Paras and Akshi had both poured out their thoughts and feelings, creating a space for honesty and healing.

"Paras," Akshi began, her voice softer than before, "I want you to know that I'm truly sorry for how I treated you in the past. I was wrong in many ways, and I should have communicated better."

Paras nodded, his expression showing a mix of understanding and relief. "Thank you, Akshi. I appreciate you saying that. It means a lot."

As they conversed, an unspoken understanding flowed between them. It was as if the weight of their past mistakes had been acknowledged, forgiven, and released into the breeze. The park, once filled with memories both sweet and bitter, now seemed to embrace their journey towards closure.

Akshi continued, "I've had time to reflect on our friendship and what it meant to me. You were always there for me, Paras, even when I didn't deserve it. I missed having you in my life."

Paras smiled faintly, appreciating her honesty. "I missed you too, Akshi. But I also needed this time to grow and figure out what I want in life."

Their eyes locked, and for a moment, it felt like the old times when they could speak volumes with just a look. But now, there was a feel a closure in the air.

"I'm glad we had this conversation, Paras," Akshi said, her voice filled with sincerity.

"Me too," Paras replied. "It's time for both of us to move forward."

They talked for a while, reminiscing about their past and sharing their current lives. It was a bittersweet conversation, but it was also necessary. As Paras walked away from the bench, he felt a wave of peace wash over him. He knew that he couldn't change the past, but he also knew that he had done what he could to make peace with it. As he made his way back home, he thought about the conversation he had with Akshi. It had been a difficult one, but he was glad they had both been able to express their feelings and come to a mutual understanding. He felt grateful for the experience, as it had taught him the importance of letting go and moving forward. And although he still had moments of sadness and nostalgia, he knew that he was on the right path towards healing. But just as he settled in at home, his phone rang.

It was Akshi. He hesitated for a moment, unsure if he was ready to talk to her again. But curiosity got the best of him, and he answered.

"Paras!" Akshi said tentatively.

"Yes Akshi, what happened you okay?" he replied, trying to keep his tone neutral.

"I just wanted to say thank you for coming. It really meant a lot to me."

Paras was surprised but pleased by her words. "Of course. I'm glad we were able to have that talk."

There was a moment of silence between them before Akshi spoke again. "I know I hurt you, Paras, and I'm sorry again. I never meant to cause you pain."

Paras felt a twinge of sadness at her words, but he also sensed a new level of sincerity in her tone.

"As I said Akshi, I appreciate your apology. Don't keep apologizing, everything is chill between us now."

There was another pause before Akshi spoke again. "Hmm, I know this might be too soon to say, but do you think there's any chance for us to try again?"

Paras was taken aback by her question. He had moved on and was in a much better place now, but a small part of him still held onto the memories of their past. But he knew that giving their relationship another chance would not be right."Akshi, I…appreciate your honesty, but I think it's better for us to move on from each other, and let's be that friends that we supposed to be later" he said firmly, but gently.

Akshi sighed, "I understand. I just had to ask. It's okay and yeah we are friends, Paras."

"Thank you, Akshi, for understanding. But remember if you need any kind of help from me, I'm always there for you."

"Thank you, paras, and same from my side too. Im just a call away."

As they hung up the phone. Paras had finally let go of the past and was ready to fully embrace the future. And with that thought, he smiled to himself, excited for whatever new adventures lay ahead. The next day, Paras woke up feeling refreshed and energized. He got dressed and headed out for a morning run, enjoying the cool breeze and the sounds of the city waking up.

As he ran, he thought about all the possibilities that lay ahead, and he felt grateful for the closure he had finally found. After his run, he headed back to his apartment to get ready for the day ahead. He had some work to catch up on, but he knew that he also needed to take some time for himself.

He decided to spend the afternoon exploring new hobbies, visiting new neighborhoods and trying out new street food. As he walked through the bustling streets, Paras felt a sense of excitement. He was ready to take on the world, to experience all the joy and beauty that life had to offer. And he knew that he was finally free to do so. The next few weeks were a blur of new experiences and adventures. Paras threw himself into his work, but he also made time for fun and exploration. He met new people, tried new foods, and explored the city in ways he never thought possible.

Sometimes closure doesn't mean a neat, tidy ending. It means finally accepting that something wasn't meant to be, and finding peace in moving on.

Finding Peace

Paras had finally come to terms with the fact that Akshi was no longer a part of his life in the way he once had been. They were now friends, and while it wasn't the same as being in a romantic relationship, Paras was grateful for Akshi's presence in his life.

He had given up on the idea of finding love again. It seemed like destiny had played its part and he was meant to be in love with Akshi, even if it didn't work out in the end. But he found solace in the fact that they could still be there for each other in a different way. Paras spent more time focusing on himself and his own personal growth.

He began to explore new hobbies and interests, and found peace in the simple things in life. He realized that happiness didn't have to come from being in a relationship, but rather from within. Through his adventures, Paras met new people who challenged him and inspired him to be his best self. He made meaningful connections with others who shared his interests and passions, and he found that his life was enriched by the diverse perspectives and experiences that his new friends brought to the table.

Despite his newfound peace, there were still moments when he missed the feeling of being in love. But he had learned to accept that it was okay to feel that way, and that it was a natural part of the healing process. As he continued to live his life with purpose and intention, Paras began to realize that he was truly happy. He didn't need a romantic relationship to feel fulfilled or complete, and he found that he was content with his life just as it was. But even as he reveled in his newfound contentment, Paras never forgot the lessons that Akshi had taught him. He knew that he had grown so much from their time together, and he was grateful for the role that she had played in his life.

One day, Paras was walking through a park when he saw a couple walking hand in hand, laughing and enjoying each other's company. For a moment, he felt a pang of sadness, but he quickly reminded himself that everyone's journey was different, and that it was okay to be on his own path. As he sat on a bench and watched the world go by, Paras realized that he had come a long way with Akshi. He had learned to let go of the past and focus on the present moment. And while he may not have found love in the way he had hoped, he had found something even more important: Inner peace.

As he walked down the street, Paras felt a renewed purpose. He realized that he had grown so much since the end of his relationship with Akshi, and he was proud of the person he had become. He started to meet new people and make new friends, slowly but surely building a support system around him.

As time went on, Paras continued to grow and evolve as a person. He worked hard at his job and found success in his career, but he never forgot to make time for the things that brought him joy. He went on hikes in the mountains and explored new cities, always eager to discover new experiences and learn more about the world around him.

He found joy in spending time with these new friends, and he realized that he was not alone in his journey. Paras also began to appreciate the beauty in the little things around him. He took walks in the park and admired the way the sun set behind the trees, he savored the taste of his favorite foods, and he relished in the feeling of the sun on his skin. He realized that he had been so focused on finding love that he had forgotten to appreciate the present moment. And now, as he focused on the here and now, he found that life was full of small pleasures that made it all worthwhile. Paras knew that he would always carry a piece of Akshi in his heart.

One day, as he was sitting in a coffee shop, Paras received a call from an unknown number. When he answered, he was surprised to hear Akshi's voice on the other end of the line. She was calling to congratulate him on his recent success at work, and as they spoke, Paras realized that the feelings he had for her had truly transformed into a deep and abiding friendship.

"Hey, Paras! It's been a while since we talked. How have you been?" Akshi's voice was warm and friendly, and Paras felt a pang of nostalgia as he heard it.

"I've been doing great, Akshi. How about you?" Paras replied, trying to keep his voice steady. Even though they were just friends now, he couldn't help but feel nervous whenever he spoke to her.

"I've been good too. I actually called to congratulate you on the big project you just completed. I heard it was a huge success!" Akshi's voice was full of excitement and genuine pride for Paras.

"Thank you so much, Akshi. It was a lot of hard work, but I'm glad it paid off in the end." Paras felt happy knowing that Akshi was still interested in his life and accomplishments.

"I'm really proud of you, Paras. You've come so far since we first met." Akshi's words were sincere, and he relieved comfort in the familiar tone of their conversation.

"Thanks, Akshi. I couldn't have done it without your support along the way." Paras felt a rush of gratitude towards Akshi. Despite their past, she had always been there for him in some way or another.

"That's what friends are for."

They both knew that they still cared for each other deeply, but they also knew that their lives were taking them in different directions. He felt a warmth in his heart. He realized that he had truly moved on from his past relationship and was ready to reconnect with Akshi as a friend. A peace in his heart as he knew that their paths might cross again someday, but for now, he was content with the memories they had shared and the closure they had finally achieved.

As they said their goodbyes and hung up the phone with a peace and contentment in his heart. But as he looked back on his past experiences and the lessons he had learned; he knew that he was ready for whatever the future had in store. With an optimism and excitement for the possibilities that lay ahead, Paras stepped out into the world once again, eager to embrace all of the joys and challenges that life had to offer.

"Sometimes, letting go of a love that wasn't meant to be is the first step towards finding inner peace and embracing the future."

Letting go of a past love can be one of the most difficult things to do. It can feel like a loss of a part of oneself, and the thought of starting over can be overwhelming. But sometimes, holding onto a love that wasn't meant to be can lead to unnecessary pain and suffering. It can hold us back from fully embracing the present moment and moving forward towards new opportunities.

Letting go is not about forgetting or dismissing the past, but rather about acknowledging it and finding a way to make peace with it. It's about allowing oneself to feel the pain and sadness, but also recognizing that those feelings will eventually pass. It's about understanding that the past cannot be changed, but the future is full of endless possibilities. When we let go of a past love, we open ourselves up to new experiences, new people, and new possibilities.

We create space for growth and personal development. And while it may be scary at first, it can also be incredibly liberating and empowering. Ultimately, letting go of a love that wasn't meant to be is a powerful act of self-love and self-care. It allows us to prioritize our own well-being and happiness, and to embrace the future with an open heart.

In Life, we often think that it shouldn't end like this. We expect the sun to shine bright, flowers to bloom. But sometimes the day turns dark and leaves us disappointed. Not because there's no daylight, but because we all want a perfect ending. We forget that in real life, reality is mostly far different from our imagination. Here, the verse of life doesn't always rhyme, and beats of life. Life simply doesn't begin or end. Life goes on. You still breathe, you still care, you still live.